Art of Public Speaking

Published by :
Lotus Press Publishers & Distributors

Art of
Public Speaking

A K. Batra

4735/22, Prakash Deep Building
Ansari Road, Darya Ganj,
New Delhi - 110002

Lotus Press : Publishers & Distributors
Unit No. 220, 2nd Floor, 4735/22, Prakash Deep Building,
Ansari Road, Darya Ganj, New Delhi- 110002
Ph.: 41325510, 98118-38000
• E-mail : lotuspress1984@gmail.com
www.lotuspress.co.in

Art of Public Speaking

ISBN: 81-8382-138-3

Printed & Published by : **Lotus Press Publishers & Distributors,** New Delhi-02

PREFACE

Public speaking involves speaking to a group of people in a structured, effective manner intended to inform, influence, or entertain the listeners. In public speaking, as in any form of communication, there are five basic elements, often expressed as "who is saying what to whom using what medium with what effects."

The motive behind public speaking can be simply transmitting information, motivating people to act, or simply telling a story. Good speakers should be able to have an impact on their listeners, not just inform them.

A speaker may address a large assembly of people or small gatherings. For large assemblies, the speaker will usually require a public address system or microphone and speaker.

Preparing and delivering your first public speech can be a daunting affair. You may be undecided about what you want to say, how to say it, or perhaps the thought of speaking before an audience scares you. Doubtless some people are naturally talented at public speaking, but have no fear—with some helpful guidance, you can write and deliver a successful speech that will be remembered for all the right reasons.

You may be tempted to sit down with a pen and paper and quickly dash off the first line of your speech. Don't. In order to save yourself a lot of time and effort, as also much frustrating re-writing, begin instead by devoting some time to careful planning of your speech. Through effective preparation, you will answer all the questions and doubts about your speech before they arise. The contents of your speech, and how you deliver it, are based on three important factors: The Occasion, The Audience, and The Purpose of Your Speech.

The nature of the occasion will obviously have a great bearing on your speech. The occasion will dictate not only the content of your speech, but also the duration, the tone, and the expectations of your audience. For example, humour may be inappropriate during a business presentation or a eulogy, while it may be welcome during a wedding speech, or a sports event. You should also be aware of your role and any observances that you should make during your speech (For example, a Best Man ought to close his speech with a toast to the Bride and Groom).

Be mindful of the occasion and your role in it.

Whatever the occasion, your speech must always be targeted at your audience.

If you are familiar with your audience, for example, if the occasion is a large family gathering, then your speech should acknowledge and build upon your existing intimacy with your audience. The use of names and personal details of members of your audience can help to engage your listeners.

By setting out a few clear goals before you start writing your speech, you will be better equipped to judge its progress and success of your speech prior to its public airing. A hilarious Best Man speech may have your audience rolling in the aisles, but if you fail to give tribute to the Bride and Groom you will have failed in your role.

By setting clear goals, you will be better positioned to judge the likely success of your speech.

Don't overcomplicate your speech. A short, impactful message with a few key points can be much better than a long-winded, rambling speech with too many (or no clear) points.

Relevant speeches are good speeches—if it matters to the audience, then they will listen.

Convey a positive attitude and bring energy to your speech. People will likely remember this (if nothing else) and this can cause the central message of your speech to be better received.

It is very important that you pay attention to even the smallest details. You can never overplan. Remember, "He who fails to plan is planning for failure"

CONTENTS

1 Plan and Assess Your Speech

Planning and preparing an informative speech can be intimidating, especially if you're relatively new to formal public speaking.

Relevant speeches are good speeches—if it matters to the audience, then they will listen.

Make sure that you convey a positive attitude and bring dynamism to your speech. People will most probably remember this (if nothing else), and this will perhaps cause the central message of your speech to be better received.

How to Choose a Good Topic

You may be invited to deliver a speech to an august gathering. You have to choose what you want to say to the audience. There are many strategies for choosing a good topic. Opt for a topic that is exciting or interesting to you, so that you can be enthusiastic about your topic while delivering your speech. But ensure that you have some prior knowledge about the topic, or at least be motivated to research the topic closely.

Select a topic that is appropriate for the situation and venue, and is a good match for your audience's interests and desires. Also ensure that the topic is specific enough and brief and not rambling. You only have a limited amount of time to give your speech, and so you can't cover everything. Identify a specific, targeted purpose and stick with it.

Knowing Your Audience

It is essential to determine whom you are going to address. In order to elicit the best response from them, you need to determine (to the best of your ability) their interests and current knowledge on the subject matter.

Some questions to consider about your audience:

a) How big an audience are you expecting?
b) What are their interests?
c) Does the audience consist primarily of certain types of people?
d) What is important to them?
e) Do you already have a relationship with audience members or does rapport need to be built up?

Rehearsing the Speech

As the saying goes, practice makes a man perfect. In order for a speech to sound natural and not stilted or canned, it is important to practise, practise, practise. You have to become as familiar with your speech as possible so that you are comfortable with the material, and can become flexible while delivering the speech.

Try answering hypothetical questions so as to get a sense of the time you should set aside for the real thing. Practise your speech several times, becoming less notes-reliant over time. Treat the speech like a conversation for greater rapport.

Planning Your Speech

Planning your speech is where the fun begins! In your imagination you may hear yourself being stunning, the audience clapping wildly...then rising to their feet to give you a standing ovation. You may see yourself being congratulated and offered several speaking contracts. Obviously they are all lucrative but you choose the one with optional extras: an extended holiday in a lovely health resort!

Consider the Occasion

How long will your speech last? Will you be the keynote speaker or one of many? Has your audience heard you before and what is their impression of you and your organisation? Is this talk one of many or a single presentation?

Journalists commonly address the questions: Who did What? When? Where? Why? How? The same questions can be starting points for selecting and organising a topic for an informative speech.

Armed with the *Who* you are going to speak for, *What* the general or specific subject matter is, How long the speech is to be and *When and Where* it is you now are ready to make a rough outline. This will be your beginning guide. You will probably alter it as you go along, as better or different ideas occur to you. That's good. It shows you're flexible and thinking. But what is important is to start the process.

On a piece of paper or in a word document on your computer write these headings with enough space between them for notes:

a) WHO
b) WHAT
c) HOW
d) WHEN
e) WHERE

a) Who

Before you commence talking, it is essential that you consider carefully your audience. What do they think about you? If you are representing a profession, agency, organisation, what does your audience think about that group?

Have you ever addressed this audience in the past? If so, what did you learn about their needs and expectations? If this is a new group to you, how will you establish your rapport and your credibility?

Note down as much as you know about the audience. This will give you ideas of what they will want to hear and be interested in. It will also serve you when it comes to shaping your material.

Your notes may read like this:

— Approximately 50 people
— Mostly in the 20's
— All working youngsters
— Mixed ethnic background but all speak English
— Hostel dwellers
— Mostly work in a campus
— Many have joined work recently
— Interested in achieving work/life balance for themselves and in particular a better financial situation

b) What

What are you speaking about? What is your topic for the presentation?

Often, as a perceived expert on a subject, this is a part of your speaking request. Sometimes, you will be invited to talk about anything within your expertise.

What is the topic you have chosen for your talk? What experience and expertise have you? What are your personal concerns and convictions?

After jotting down the topics for which you have interest and experience, begin to talk with colleagues to clarify your position.

Write down the title and/or type of speech you have been asked to prepare.

Next, using your notes from the WHO section of your headings, begin another set. Now your objective is to see how what you know or have been asked to talk about can be specifically shaped to meet and serve the interests of your audience.

Let's look at an example.

You have been asked to give a motivational speech to the group identified above. The organiser wants you to share your life story as a guide or inspiration. Your background is similar to many of the employees you will be speaking to. You came as an apprentice, and had communication problems with your seniors due to poor command over your English language. You attended English courses conducted by the company where you had to interact with the other members in the group in English.

So how do you shape your story to fit your audience? You don't want to overwhelm them with information so they can't think straight or digest it. That will turn them off. They will think it's too difficult and beyond them. They may listen, be interested but they won't identify with it. You want them to feel they can take from your experience and use it to enrich their own lives.

What you have noted down is not a speech yet but you can see the beginnings of its shape and how you have used your knowledge of the audience to ensure giving them something they'll enjoy listening to and identify with.

c) How

The next agenda from your list is to tackle the 'how'. There are two important 'how's'. The first is how long the speech is to be. The time you have been given will determine what you put into your speech and what you will leave out. If you have a relatively short time (10 minutes), you will need to either focus on one major topic with examples to illustrate, or settle for covering a maximum of three lightly. The purpose of your speech and your audience will help you make the most relevant choice. A longer time gives you more freedom to develop several themes fully.

The second 'how' relates to the method of presentation. For example: Will this be a speech told with humour? Will you use visual aids? (This is when you take objects relevant to your speech to illustrate your points. It could be photographs or items if they are suitable to transport.) Could you give a demonstration?

While pondering on this 'how' keep in mind the different needs of your audience. Most people have a preferred mode for receiving information. Some people understand well through listening. They are called 'auditory'. Some people get most of their understanding through looking. They are called 'visual'. Others receive and understand information best when they can touch, feel or do what is being explained to them. These are the 'kinesthetics'. A considerate and effective speaker tries to include all three modes in his speech.

Remember that the 'how' heading will depend on the time available. If it is short you may have to leave out demonstrations but you will always be able to include something to meet all three modes satisfactorily.

Suppose you have just 10 minutes time at your disposal. How to present?

Definitely with humour!

d) When

Are you to be the first in a long line of speakers? For symposium presentations or public speaking classes, this is common. If you are the tenth of twenty speakers, you can imagine the boredom that your audience might have.

If you are the keynote speaker, your host will introduce you to the audience. He is expected to warm up the audience, to clarify the purpose of the occasion and to help you establish your credibility.

An important aspect of public speaking is the duration of your talk. Try to end your talk before your audience has stopped listening. Very few audience members will complain that a speaker talked too briefly—more will complain that the speaker talked too long.

Consider also the time, day and season of the speech that will have an impact on what you do and say. For example: You can use the early bird start in the middle of winter on a wet Monday morning effectively by acknowledging the efforts people have made to be there! With a little bit of thinking you'll find ways of tying in what is happening in the 'here and now' with your content. A word of warning: Be conscious of presenting difficult or challenging material when people are either both tired and hungry (just before lunch or dinner) or when they've just eaten! Concentration spans are not at their best in either situation. If possible save this type of content for a mid-morning or afternoon slot.

e) Where

Another aspect to be taken into consideration is the physical environment. Points to consider are: Where will I be in relation to the audience? Will they see me easily? Will they hear me easily? Do I need a microphone? Is there a place to put my notes if I'm using some? Are there power points if I want to use any electronic devices? Do I have to provide everything I want to use (e.g.: computer, screen…)? Many fully prepared, beautifully rehearsed speeches fail because insufficient thought has gone into where they are to take place. It's no fun when people can neither see nor hear you or the carefully thought through demonstration is stymied through lack of a power point in the right place!

Clarifying the Goal

When asked to speak, there are three major purposes to consider:

1) Talking to inform
2) Speaking to entertain
3) Talking to persuade

If the purpose of your speech is to be informative, your goal is to present new information for the enlightenment of your audience. Informative talks may include speeches to demonstrate how something works or how to do something. We expect these talks to be balanced and objective. Many university lectures are informative briefings.

Communication experts George Grice and John Skinner suggest that you serve as mentor when you speak to inform; as advocate when you speak to persuade (to convince or to actuate) and as entertainer when you speak to amuse your audience.

Once you have a sense of your subject, it's time to limit the scope of it.

Putting the Plan Together

Once you have got all the notes ready, rearrange them and re-write until the outline is clear. After completion of this part, you'll be ready to do any research required and then you're on to the task of writing your speech.

Make very sure that your speech is short, sweet and simple. There's nothing magical about it — just methodical one-step-after-another planning. If you find yourself confused and flustered, go back to the core headings and ask yourself the key questions once more.

— WHO is this speech for?
— WHAT am I going to tell them that is relevant and interesting?
— HOW long is the speech expected to be?
— HOW am I going to present it?
— WHEN is the speech for? (date, day, time, season)

— WHERE is the speech going to happen? (hall, outdoors, stadium, school, etc.)

Write your answers down and let them be your guide. Remember this is not your finished speech. It's your outline—a guide to what you're going to cover. Don't spend too much time trying to get it perfect. You'll want that energy for researching, writing and rehearsing!

Find a Topic

In many circumstances, the topic of your talk is already apparent to you. You want to speak before a community group to change a policy. You've been asked to give a speech at an inaugural function. Your boss is retiring and you'd like to honour him. Or you are sharing your recommendations for improving a procedure to make your work more efficient.

What do you want to talk about? What experience and expertise have you? What are your personal concerns and convictions?

Develop a long list of possibilities; listen to the media and read; keep up with current news; clarify your speaking goal What is the pupose of your talk? Have you been invited to share your expertise on a topic? Will you be celebrating a special occasion or presenting an award? Do you seek to motivate your audience to make a change? Or are you merely talking to entertain?

In short, ensure that your topic is worthwhile, appropriate, culturally sensitive and limited in scope.

When and What to Research

Once you already know your subject thoroughly, inside out, back to front and sideways, there will be no need to research. But if you don't, the outline should point to the gaps needing to be filled up with specific information.

Careful research adds authority to your work. It shows care, thought and dedication to getting it right. Your audience will appreciate and respect you for it.

It is important that if you are presenting material as fact rather than as opinion, check it! Make sure you know rather than think you know.

Setting Your Personal Speaking Goals

Professional speakers learn a lot from each other. They realise the importance of honing their skills on a regular basis and often work with speaker coaches. Whether you are a professional speaker, or someone just starting as a speaker it is important to constantly improve what you do.

Maybe your goal is to develop a new or additional topic to speak on. Maybe your goal is to become a professional speaker or maybe your goal is to speak more than you did last year. Maybe your goal is to learn how to use the internet more effectively.

In any event, take the time to reflect on what you did this past year and write down what you hope to achieve this year.

2 Analyse Your Audience

For any public speaker, it is essential to analyse the demographic, psychographic and situational characteristics of his audience.

Just as a gardener must tend to the individual needs of each plant, a speaker must know his audience well. Learn all that you can about your audience in order to meet the needs of your speaking occasion.

Demographic Characteristics of Your Audience

It is always useful to consider the possible areas of diversity in an audience. These characteristics may include:

a) Age
b) Gender
c) Ethnicity, race, and cultural background
d) Education
e) Religious and political affiliations
f) Economic status
g) Sexual orientation
h) Family background
i) Group membership

Psychographic Characteristics of Your Audience

Consider the psychological profiles of your audience as you shape your message. These may include:

a) Beliefs are opinions held by many.
b) Values are views of the goodness/badness or sense of right or wrong.

c) Attitudes are predispositions to behaviour such as inclination to vote.
d) Behaviors are actions taken. These are not always consistent with beliefs, values and attitudes.
e) Situational characteristics of your talk.
f) Situational factors that affect your presentation include the time, audience size, location and occasion of the talk.

The members in the audience tend to be more alert in the late morning and in the middle of the week. Speaking first or last helps you to get better evaluations.

Ensure that there are no environmental distractions that can negatively affect your audience—the lighting, temperature, sitting arrangement, and general mood of the audience.

Self-assessment of Credibility

Given below are questions that will help you determine how credible your audience perceives you to be. You can also reflect on how to adapt your speech so that your credibility will be enhanced.

Your credibility is established when you are viewed as possessing competence and confidence to speak on the subject; when your audience respects your moral character and trustworthiness; and if your listeners see you as relating to them by creating goodwill.

1. Are you competent and confident to speak on the subject?

The audience will judge you by the perception that you know what you are talking about in the light of your education, professional experience and the research you've done on the topic. You create that perception by explicitly identifying how you developed your knowledge to speak on the subject. Competence may also be affected by the topic and how much the audience is predisposed to agree or disagree with you. The perception that you are confident in your knowledge is further communicated through dynamic and smooth delivery.

a) What is the topic for your persuasive speech?
b) What is your specific persuasive goal?
c) To what degree do you think your audience agrees with that goal?

In general the greater the degree of resistance for most members of the audience, the more will you need to provide a significant amount of credible evidence. In the light of the audience position on your topic, you should do the following to enhance the audience perception of your competence:

i) describe your personal experience and background relevant to the topic
ii) describe your professional training or academic work related to the topic
iii) use a significant amount of evidence from highly credible sources and build the credibility of your evidence by explaining the credentials of the sources that you will cite in your speech.

You can work on the following elements of delivery to enhance the perception of confidence by:

i) using more eye contact and direct communication with the audience.
ii) enhancing your vocal variety by using natural modifications of rate, pitch and loudness.
iii) using silent pauses rather than vocalised pauses such as "uhm", "ah" and "uh".
iv) maintaining a more stable posture and home base.
v) using movement and gestures selectively, purposefully and naturally to reinforce main ideas.

2. *What does the audience think of your character and trustworthiness?*

Perceptions of character and trust are value judgements of you and your topic. You create the sense of character by stressing personal values that you share with your listeners. Trust is also earned by demonstrating that you have acted and spoken in a reliable and consistent manner.

Are there any significant moral reservations that your listeners may have about your topic that might affect their perception of your character and trustworthiness? Explain.

Which of the following values do you think you share with the audience? Check as many as apply.

i) My Values
ii) My Audience's Values
iii) Honesty
iv) taking responsibility
v) ambitious and hard working
vi) willing to forgive others
vii) open minded and tolerant
viii) courageous in standing up for others
ix) helpful and showing concern for the welfare of others
x) loving and affectionate
xi) capable and effective

On which values do you have the greatest convergence with your audience? Explain how you can stress in your speech that you and your audience share the same values.

3. *How does the audience perceive you in matters of goodwill and confidence?*

Goodwill and rapport are achieved by stressing that you share common experiences, interests and concerns with your audience. Your listeners may also feel a greater sense of rapport with you on the basis of demographic factors.

a) What are some of the shared experiences that you can allude to in your speech?
b) How does your speech address the interests, needs and concerns of your audience?
c) Which of the following demographic factors create common ground between you and your audience? Check all that apply.

i) age
ii) sex
iii) educational level
iv) social class
v) family background

Explain how you will create identification with your audience on the basis of shared demographics.

Notwithstanding differences, how will you stress common ground with your audience in order to create goodwill?

Consider cultural considerations. Ignoring cultural differences and expectations is considered rude and impolitic.

Consider cultural differences. As you probably know, the rules and expectations for communicating well differ from culture to culture. There are many people who tend to expect direct communication, so speakers are likely to get right to the point and state their thesis during the introduction of the talk. Many other cultures, including those that are considered collectivistic, consider the directness of such people as blunt and inconsiderate. For many African and South American cultures, speakers are expected to be more subtle and less direct than US Americans. Many Asian cultures believe that maintaining social harmony is far more important than directness. Likewise, the Mexican culture prefers indirect politeness to the US manner of speaking.

Joseph DeVito offers the following suggestions drawn from the Task Force on Bias-Free Language of the Association of

American University Presses for avoiding sexism, heterosexism and racism:

1. *Woman or young woman* is preferred to girl or lady when referring to an adult female;
2. *Older person* is preferred to *elder, senior* or *senior citizen*;
3. *Gay and lesbian refers to a lifestyle. Sexual orientation is preferred to sexual preference;*
4. Most African Americans prefer *African American to black;*
5. *White* is used to refer to European Americans;
6. *Hispanic* refers to a person from a Spanish-speaking culture. *Latina* (female) and *Latino* (male) refer to Latin American cultures.
7. *Inuk* (plural of Inuit) is preferred to Eskimo;
8. *American Indian* is preferred to *Native American;*
9. *Muslim* is now preferable to *Moslem*;
10. *Jewish people is preferred to Jew (male) and* Jewess (female); and *Asian* is preferred to *Oriental.*

But not all agree on how to handle and address the complications of cultural differences. Interact with your audience during your talk. All speakers seek to converse with their audience members in order to reach them. As you are delivering your talk, consider adopting a heightened conversational tone.

Begin your talk with a "non-verbal handshake". In the U.S. American culture, this means that you make eye contact with as many audience members as you can. This means making contact long enough to discern whether your message is clear and interesting. As you make contact, you will be able to show that you care about what effect your words and movements have upon your audience. Make sure that you smile a genuine smile that conveys your sincere welcome and appreciation for their attention.

Adult audiences will want:

a) To be given information that they can use immediately;
b) To be actively involved in the learning process;
c) To connect their life experiences with the new information they learn; and
d) To know how the new information is relevant to their needs and their busy lives.

When you are in a conversation with another, you will receive feedback about the effect that your message is having. You know to adapt your message accordingly. Do the same with public speaking.

Because it is in your audience's best interests for you to succeed, participants will give you feedback before, during, and following your talk. This is where excellent listening skills come into play.

Like a good conversation, the first thing that you do when greeting your audience is to establish rapport and find common areas of interest. Introduce yourself and clearly state your purpose and rationale for choosing the topic and thesis that you have for this talk.

If you are willing to take questions during your talk, invite your audience to interrupt you. If you plan to talk for 20 minutes and then take 10 minutes for questions and comments, make that clear as well. This gives your audience a clear sense of how you expect to interact with them.

Get Feedback Following Your Talk

While you are rehearsing your talk, you'll want to be sure to solicit feedback from family and colleagues. Following you talk, be sure to debrief the presentation as well.

In a public speaking course, you will have the advantage of receiving feedback from skilled evaluators including your instructor. Your professor has been given specific training in watching and evaluating talks and is likely to offer you balanced, specific, and constructive criticism.

In addition, you will probably have your presentation videotaped. Watch it at least three times. The first viewing will not be friendly for you will likely see all the physical characteristics that you don't like about your delivery or your appearance. Most speakers dislike their voices, their movements, their hair and their weight when they watch the videotapes. This is normal! Watch the video again!

The second time that you view your video, you will likely notice that you don't appear to be as nervous as you were feeling. Looking composed is a positive thing! Seek to get past your delivery and notice how well you engage your audience with genuine, positive and organised manner.

When you watch your video a third time, you are likely to begin to see yourself in the same way that your audience saw you. This is a more objective and useful tool for assessing your presentation.

It is useful to solicit feedback from your classmates as well. Learn from them how well you adapted your talk to meet their specific expectations and needs. Ask for both positive feedback and suggestions for future improvements.

Self-assess Your Presentation

Opening

1. Did you greet your audience and introduce yourself?
2. Did you establish your credibility?
3. Was your thesis statement clearly stated at the start of your talk?
4. Did you orient your audience to your format and clarify how you wanted to handle interruptions (e.g., questions and comments)?
5. Did your presentational style enhance the briefing?

Body

1. Was the talk well organised?
2. Were your main points clear?
3. Did your talk flow logically from one point to the next?
4. Were the judgments substantiated?
5. Was your support accurate, brief, and clear?
6. Did your visual aids clearly enhance the briefing and reinforce your main points?

Conclusion

7. Did you cue your audience that you were concluding your talk?
8. Did you succinctly re-emphasize your key points and your thesis?
9. Did you clearly present the implication for your audience concerning this issue?
10. Did you thank your audience for listening?

Question and Answer

1. Did you handle questions directly, succinctly and tactfully?

Delivery

1. Did you control your nervousness?
2. Did you make eye contact with your audience?
3. Did you speak in a conversational tone?
4. Did you avoid using jargon or other language barriers?
5. Were your gestures, facial expressions, and body movements consistent with your message?
6. Did you talk with your audience, rather than at them?

Impromptu or Extemporaneous Speaking

While many of us do not like to speak in front of people, there are times when we are asked to get up and say a few words about someone or a topic when we have not planned on saying anything at all. We are more shocked than anyone else. Has this ever happened to you? If and when this does happen to you, be prepared to rise to the challenge. Below are some tips you can use the next time you are called on to speak.

Decide quickly what your one message will be. Keep in mind you have not been asked to give a speech but to make some impromptu remarks. Hopefully they have asked you early enough so you can at least jot down a few notes before you speak. If not, pick ONE message or comment and focus on that one main idea. Many times, other ideas may come to you after you start speaking. If this happens, go with the flow and trust your instincts.

Do not try and memorise what you will say. Trying to memorise will only make you more nervous and you will find yourself thinking more about the words and not about the message.

Start off strong and with confidence. If you at least plan your opening statement, this will get you started on the right foot. After all, just like with any formal speech, getting started is the most difficult. Plan what your first sentence will be. You may even write this opening line down on your note card and glance at it one more time just before you begin speaking. If you know you have three points or ideas to say, just start off simple by saying, "I would just like to talk about 3 points". The first point is... the second point is... and so on.

Decide on your transitions from one point to the other. After you have decided on your opening remark or line, come up with a simple transition statement that takes you to your main point. If you have more than one point to make, you can use a natural transition such as, "My second point is... or my next point is..." etc. Just list on your note card or napkin, if you have to, the main points or ideas. Do not write out the exact words, but just the points you want to mention.

Maintain eye contact with the audience. This is easier to do if you do not write down all kinds of stuff to read. Look down at your next idea or thought and maintain eye contact with your audience and speak from your heart. Focus on communicating TO your audience and not speaking AT the crowd.

Occasionally throw in an off-the-cuff remark. Because you want your style to be flexible and seem impromptu, trust your instinct and add a few words that just pop into your head. Keep it conversational and think of the audience as a group of your friends.

Finally, have a good conclusion. Gracefully just state, "And the last point I would like to make is...." Once you have made your last point, you can then turn control back to the person who asked you to speak in the first place.

With a little practice, this process will feel more natural to you. Anticipating that you may be asked to say a few words should force you to at least think about what you might say if you are asked. Then if you are asked, you are better prepared because you anticipated being asked. This is much better than thinking they won't ask you and they actually do!

3 Research Your Topic

Develop Your Expertise

You want to be perceived by your audience as an expert in your subject. Experience, knowledge, and integrity are keys to developing your expertise.

According to DeVito, competence refers to the knowledge and expertise an audience thinks you have.

Whenever possible, select a topic for which you have direct experience. Tell your story.

Be sure that you are well researched. Even if you have a great deal of experience, you need to consult with other experts to ensure that your knowledge is generalizable and consistent. If your experience is different from that of many others, you have a responsibility to share that too.

Cite a variety of research sources to demonstrate that you are objective, reliable and balanced in your reasoning. Cite your sources throughout your talk and clarify the expertise of these sources as well. By referencing other experts, you will enhance your own credibility by sharing your competence. Watch newscasters to hear how to provide oral footnotes. For instance, you'll probably say, "According to..." often.

The following tips may be useful for using citing expert opinions:

1. Be certain that any authority you cite as an expert is an expert on the subject you are discussing.

2. Identify your sources to ensure that your audience understands that the sources are well qualified.
3. Cite unbiased authorities.
4. Cite opinions that are representative of prevailing opinions.
5. Quote your sources accurately.
6. Use literary quotations sparingly.

Boost Your Credibility

Work with other experts to boost your credibility. Even the most expert of us recognises that there are many perspectives and ways to look at a topic. Good speakers ensure that they are up-to-date and aware of what other experts are doing in their field.

Work with Other Experts

If you are a college student, you have a vast number of professional experts available to you! Be sure to take advantage of your easy access to these experts to learn the current research and suggestions for making your presentation credible.

In addition, there are professional organisations for nearly every subject imaginable. For example, the communication field has a number of professional organisations for those interested in networking with other communication experts.

Beyond the university are a number of research institutes called, "think tanks". Some are conversative, others quite liberal so be sure to explore several to get balanced perspectives.

Assess the Credibility of Resources

As you know, there are many of people who pretend to be experts on subjects for which they know little. In addition, some misrepresent the facts or fabricate evidence.

Imagine that you want to give a talk about the importance of developing and maintaining a good financial credit history. There are a number of resources available to you. Banks, stores, even universities offer credit cards that enable one to go into debt. Doubtlessly, family and friends maintain credit card, so can give you suggestions. Your task as a researcher is to determine which of the resources are the most credible.

Which of the following would most likely be reliable, objective, and expert?

Your friend neighborhood banker, or your cousin who has four credit cards and a $4,000 debt?

Well, it's possible that you'd get good advice from a friendly banker. And you might be advised about what not to do by a cousin in financial trouble. There are sites that give you practical tips on how card companies target students, why we want credit cards, how they're billed, the pitfalls of owning them, and how to recover after mistakes.

Evaluating Sources of Information on the Web

As you sort through the volume of information available on the Web, it is critical to make assessments about the accuracy and reliability of the information you find.

How to Research

The key to how to research efficiently is to know who and what you're looking for! Sounds simple? Sometimes it is and sometimes it's a challenge. But the great news is you use research skills constantly whether you know it or not! The fact you're here now is testimony to them being alive and well, and working for you. You put keywords into a search engine and you came up with this page, didn't you?

How to research are part of the bundle of skills making your life efficient. You probably wouldn't go to an unfamiliar city looking for a particular street without a map; otherwise you'd be running round in circles for months, if not years. The same principle is true of researching for a specific speech or presentation subject.

Generally getting relevant information is a matter of using sound common sense, i.e., the 'how to research' skills you already have! If you want to find out about something you go to the places where that information is most likely to be.

So how does this work in practice with a speech topic?

The starting point of 'how to research' is always to know as much as possible about your audience.

Knowing your audience will give you a fairly accurate gauge of the degree of complexity or depth required to meet their needs. Now combine this information with the length of time you're expected to fill and the brief (subject and purpose of the speech) you've been given (if any).

The result of: audience + time + brief = an indication of the research requirements.

When you have this sorted you're on your way in the 'how to research' process.

The next step is to find out how much you already know about where to get the information you need to support your topic authoritatively. Grab the outline you made as you went through the planning page and look it again.

You will have noted down your topic heading (what it is you are going to speak about) and several (1, 2, 3 or more) main ideas or sub-headings. Each one of these gives important information and you'll want to support it with good examples.

The next step of 'how to research' is not to go rushing off to the library or on to the net but to go systematically through your sub-headings, making yourself notes about what you need to research and where you think you'll find it. If you already have the information at your fingertips, jot that down too. This will save you time by making your researching targeted.

The main information location areas are libraries and internet. Other sources are:

a) International, national and local authorities/ organisations (reachable through either their internet site or telephone book listing)
b) Newspapers (again often available online)
c) Magazines(try online for these too)
d) Radio/TV(also often online)
e) Specific specialist resource people(interviews)

Using the internet is a superb place to start. There is so much information buzzing around out there just waiting to be culled and researched. And that's part of its challenge. To avoid spending hours sifting through endless websites to finish with nothing, use a few 'how to research' on the internet tricks.

1. Use distinctive phrases rather than general terms to narrow the results, e.g., 'effects of cigarette smoking' rather than 'cigarettes' or 'cigarette smoking'.
2. If you know the proper name of the organisation or person enter it
3. Use AND to link two or more subjects together, e.g., children AND reading AND success.
4. Be aware of different spellings, synonyms or alternate forms you could use for your search term.
5. Try using speech marks around your phrase e.g. "children AND reading AND success"
6. Different search engines have different methods of retrieving results. If you're not getting what you want, try finding out how to research for the specific engine you're using by clicking up their help pages.

Having found web pages offering information you want, evaluate them. The internet is a self-publishing paradise. Anybody can put up a website and they're generally free to say whatever they like on whatever subject! So before you leap and grab the first 'authority' fitting your topic, look carefully. Is the website believable? How do you know? Is this one person's voice and if so, whose is it? What are his/her credentials? Is this an official organisation's site? Are contact details available?

A rule of thumb 'how to research' tip is to gather more than one reputable website. Three makes a reasonable sample. If they all are saying similar things about your topic, you can probably safely assume the information is valid. If you want more information than is available on site, use the contact page and send an email. You may or may not be rewarded with a response but a polite detailed enquiry outlining who you are, what information you want and the purpose for asking is worth a try!

To easily collect the information for future reference, copy and paste into a word document. Remember to take the url as well and bookmark the sites before leaving them as you may have to return to get further information.

How to Research from a Library

There are bonuses to the library not available on the internet. These are that you get live people (librarians) to talk to and real books to handle!

Use a similar 'how to research' system as on the internet.

Enter the details of your subject into the library online database, and again the more specific you can be, the more likelihood you'll find what you want. The results will let you know what material is held where and direct you to find it.

If you can't find what you want ask a librarian how to research using the library's system. They enjoy being involved in ensuring people get what they need.

If you are confronted by a large number of different books and perhaps magazine or newspaper articles as well, use the rapid scan technique.

For a book or magazine flip open the contents page and quickly read the chapter or article headings. If there's an index at the back of the book search out your key words. Nothing? Put the books back. Something? Check them out to take home for closer reading.

How to Research Using the Telephone Book

If you have the name of either an organisation or a person who could supply the information you need, ring them! You'll need to judge for yourself the possible pay-off compared to the costs involved. These could be in time, and money depending where the person or organisation is in relation to you.

Tips for Top Telephone Results

1. Don't dial the number before preparing.
2. Write yourself a list of the questions you want to ask.
3. Be as specific as possible.
4. Rank your questions from most important to least.
5. Gauge how much time you are asking for. If you've prepared 30 minutes of question and answer, a busy person may not have that to give you!
6. Have a piece of paper and pen handy for writing down the answers.
7. If possible know at least a little about the organisation and /or person before ringing.
8. If you're ringing a large organisation and don't know who to ask for, ask the receptionist who would be the most suitable person to talk to you about your topic. Get their name and ask if they are available.
9. If so, introduce yourself, state your purpose, i.e., collecting information for a speech to be given to so and so in two weeks' time, ask if they have enough time to talk to you.

10. If you get the go ahead, ask your questions and carefully record the answers.
11. Be sure to thank the person for their time.
12. If the person is not able to answer your questions right away, ask if there is a time when you could call back.

Collating your Results

Collating your material can be a breeze or a mission. It depends on you.

Mission people are those who have to read everything and then have to re-evaluate their outline to see if they're missing something they simply must put in. Once they start to re-evaluate they begin to question their choices. They doubt they've followed the 'how to research' process correctly.

It's called wanting to make it perfect and while that's good in smallish doses, too much saps your confidence. The end result of 'too much' is paralysis. You end up blocked and anxious, and finally, scrambling to honour your deadline. Avoid it. If you can, catch yourself doing it and STOP.

If you've done your homework and found out what your audience expects and wants, then you do understand. You simply need get on with it rather than make it more complicated for yourself!

By contrast the breeze people sail through, cool as could be. How do they do it? They stick to their main idea headings in their original outline. They *only* take information if it supports and extends their ideas in a substantial way. If the information is off-track or of little consequence they discard it. They stop reading. They don't take notes. They move on to the next source. And they *only* read what is necessary to understand what is being said and how it fits with their speech. In other words, if you don't have to read a whole book, don't. Take the bits you need and no more. Knowing what to take and what to leave out is part of learning how to research effectively. Like most things, you'll get more efficient through practice.

How to Process Information from Print Material or a Website

Firstly collect up all your source material. Print off selected text from the websites you've book-marked and have any other material (books, newspapers, magazines, interview notes, etc.) ready for action. To speed your progress, sort them into piles matching each of your main ideas.

Write your first main idea heading at the top of a blank sheet of paper. Example: 'The Impossible Does Happen'. Now go to the 'The Impossible Does Happen' resource pile to begin processing the material.

Under the heading on your paper write the type and name of the first source.

Example: Book: *Lesser Known Facts of Flying Pigs* by John Dreamer, published by Inspired Life, 2001.

Now you can either summarise in your own words the information you need or take a direct quote from the text.

If you have more than one point to summarise rank them in order from the most important to the least.

If you wish to use a passage straight from the text without summarising, copy the section down. Note the page number (or website url, etc.), so you can return if need be.

If you have more than one source per main idea, be sure to number them as you process them.

Once you've finished working with your first main idea, start another sheet of paper for the second and third, and so on.

Be sure to keep all your pieces of paper clearly marked and together! (You'll be using them soon to write your speech.)

Keep in mind as you go of both the audience and the length of time you're speaking for. If you gather too much information you'll be unable to use it inside the time-frame. If the information is either too complex or simple, or simply not relevant, you'll have to discard it. It's easier to do the processing ahead rather than later.

Remember to always acknowledge the original speaker or writer. Most people do not mind you using their work; in fact most of them appreciate and enjoy it. But they do mind if you do not say where you got your information from or try to pass it off as your own. This is called plagiarism and can incur hefty fines if you get caught. And they mind if you twist, distort or manipulate their words to fit your own ends. Play fair...be nice. Be honest.

Gathering Information and Materials

The most difficult and also the most important part of making a presentation is actually getting started.

Your first step is to collect and read as much information as possible about your subject. Take notes.

The next step involves selecting the information and deciding how much of it you will present. To accomplish this, you need to know how long your talk will be. Naturally, the amount of material you will discuss in an hour differs from the amount you will handle in a full-day presentation; however, the format or structure should be the same in both cases.

Deciding on the format is your next step. It is at this point that you need to decide how and in what sequence you will present the material you have chosen.

Other matters to consider are:

1. What visuals will I use?
2. Where will I stand when I speak?
3. How can I present the material clearly and in an interesting fashion?

When asked to speak in public, the first things some people think about are: "What am I going to wear?", "Will there be a lot of people there?" "What if I mess up?"

These are all important questions, but they represent just a small part of what needs to be taken into consideration when preparing a presentation.

Quality Speech Material

We often ask ourselves, "What if my speech is not good enough?" If we construct our speeches with care and properly prepare and practise, our speech material will always be good.

Don't be afraid to take risks and present new material. Remember, practice makes perfect.

Speech Preparation as a Process

Genuine speech preparation means digging something out of yourself. You need to both gather facts and arrange your thoughts. It is not enough to simply collect ideas. You must also nurture them and reflect on how to present them in a unique, organised manner.

A speech needs time to grow. Prepare for weeks. Sleep on your topic, dream about it and let your ideas sink into your subconscious. Ask yourself questions. Write down your thoughts. Keep adding new ideas.

Once you've determined your purpose for delivering this speech, state the purpose in a sentence and focus your speech around that purpose. Ask yourself, "How does this purpose relate to the audience?"

Let your purpose drive your speech. Try to come up with a good title too. Aim not only to inform your listeners, but also persuade them.

As you prepare each presentation, you should develop a simple and orderly outline. You will need to decide the sequence you will follow from these organisational patterns:

1. Sequential
2. Categorical
3. Problem and solution
4. Contrast and comparison

In developing the sequence of your presentation, mind-mapping or webbing techniques can be very useful. Remember to decide, too, on the transitions between sections and examples you will use. Real-life anecdotes can be particularly effective.

The use of personal stories always works best for most audiences. Most professional speakers always use personal stories and quite often it is a personal story that becomes their "signature" story.

To be successful it is extremely important to start gathering information as soon as possible. You may ask, "How far in advance should I begin preparing for my speech?" The answer is, "You should begin preparing your speech the moment they ask you to speak!" The sooner you begin the more time you will have to practise your speech.

Mark Twain was a great speaker. In fact, he is one of the earliest known professional speakers, and when asked one day if he could prepare a speech for an upcoming engagement, he responded ,"If you want me to speak for an hour, I am ready today....If you want me to speak for just a few minutes, it will take me a few weeks to prepare."

As with most speakers, it usually takes more time to prepare a short version of a speech than a longer one. When you prepare your next speech, try preparing two—one that will run approximately one hour and one that will only run 10 minutes. You will find that Mark Twain was right. In either case, you must gather your facts and decide on what is most important.

4 Writing a Speech

Structure

Most good writing, we are told over and over again, must have a structure. A good speech is no exception. By providing your speech with a beginning, middle, and an end, you will have laid the foundations for a successful speech that fulfils all of your aspirations.

The Beginning

The first thirty seconds of your speech are probably the most important. In that period of time you must grab the attention of the audience, and engage their interest in what you have to say in your speech.

This can be achieved in several ways. For example you could raise a thought-provoking question, make an interesting or controversial statement, recite a relevant quotation or even recount a joke.

Once you have won the attention of the audience, your speech should move seamlessly to the middle of your speech.

The Body

The body of your speech will always be the largest part of your speech. At this point your audience will have been introduced to you and the subject of your speech (as set out in your opening), and will hopefully be ready to hear your arguments, your musings or on the subject of your speech.

The best way to set out the body of your speech is by formulating a series of points that you would like to raise. In the context of your speech, a "point" could be a statement about a product, a joke about the bridegroom or a fond memory of the subject of a eulogy.

The points should be organised so that related points follow one another and that each point builds upon the previous one. This will also give your speech a more logical progression, and make the job of the listener a far easier one.

Don't try to overwhelm your audience with countless points. It is better to have fewer points that you make well than to have too many points, none of which are made satisfactorily.

The Closing

Like your opening, the closing of your speech must contain some of your strongest material.

You should view the closing of your speech as an opportunity. It is an opportunity to:

a) Summarise the main points of your speech
b) Provide some further food for thought for your listeners
c) Leave your audience with positive memories of your speech
d) Choose the final thought/emotion (for example, with well wishes to the Bride and Groom, with fond memories of a departed friend, with admiration for winners and losers at an awards ceremony, etc).

Learning how to write a speech needn't be a nail-biting experience! If you can share or explain things you're interested in or passionate about then you can write a good speech.

Unsure? Don't be. Put aside your objections. You may have lived with the idea you were never good with words for a long time. Or perhaps writing papers at school brought you out in cold sweats but this is different.

Learning how to write a speech is easy when you learn to write out loud. And that's what you are going to now.

If you've done all your planning and preparation, you're set to go. You'll have a successful speech written in next to no time. But before you begin putting pen to paper or fingers to keyboard let's review to make sure you've assembled the essential ingredients.

You need to have ready:

1. Your Outline. Check your outline to make sure you have covered:
   a) WHO the speech is for
   b) WHAT the speech is to be about (main points ranked in order of importance)
   c) HOW long it needs to be and HOW you are going to present it
   d) If WHEN and WHERE are relevant include them as well
   e) The research

Got it? Great! You're ready to roll.

The Quick 'How to Write a Speech' Checklist

The basic 'how to write a speech' format is simple. It consists of three parts:

1. An opening or introduction
2. The body where the bulk of the information is given
3. An ending (or summary).

Think of it as a sandwich. The opening and ending are the slices of bread holding the filling (body) together! You can build yourself a simple sandwich with one filling or you can go gourmet and add many. The choice is yours. But whatever you choose to serve, as a good cook, you need to consider who is going to eat it! And that's your audience. So with them in mind, let's prepare the filling first.

Go to your OUTLINE where you have listed the main ideas you want to cover.

Take the most important which will be your first one to work with.

1. How to Write a Speech: Step One

Consider HOW you can explain (show, tell) that to your audience in the most appropriate way for them to easily follow and understand it.

Before you begin read the suggestions below for writing well out-loud.

A principal consideration in 'how to write a speech' is a good one is never written from the speaker's point of view. For maximum effectiveness the writer always considers the audience.

The trick here is to identify either a real person or the type of person who is most likely to be in your audience. Make sure you select someone who represents the 'majority' of your listeners. That I,s they are neither struggling to comprehend you at the bottom of your scale or light-years ahead of you at the top end. Now imagine they are sitting next to you eagerly waiting to hear what you're going to say. Give them a name, for example, Jo. It will help to make them real.

Ask yourself:

a) How do I need to tailor my information to suit Jo?
b) What type or level of language is right for Jo as well as my topic?
c) If I use jargon, will Jo understand me?

2. How to Write a Speech: Step Two

Write down what you think you'd say as if you were talking directly to them. If it helps, say everything aloud before you write or use a recorder. After you've finished, play it back and take notes. You do not have to write absolutely everything you're going to say if you don't want to, but you do need to write the sequence of thoughts to ensure they are logical and easily followed. Remember too, to explain or illustrate your point with examples from your research.

Just remember, if this is a first speech or the first of this particular type of speech the safety net of having everything written down could be just what you need. It's easier to recover from a patch of jitters when you have a full set of notes than if you have either none or a bare outline.

3. How to Write a Speech: Step Three

Refine or re-work until you're satisfied that you've made yourself clear. Do not assume that your audience will understand what you mean to say if you are not clear!

Check the 'tone' of your language. Is it right for the occasion, subject matter and your audience?

Check the length of your sentences. If they're too long or complicated you risk losing your listeners. They'll get lost trying to follow you.

Have you chosen to use words everybody will understand? Read what you've written aloud. If it flows naturally put it to one side and continue the process with your next main idea. If it doesn't flow, rework until it does.

Remember you are writing 'oral language'. You are writing as if you were explaining, telling or showing something to someone. It doesn't have to be perfect sentences. We don't talk like that. We use whole sentences and part ones and we mix them up with asides or appeals, e.g. 'Did you get that? Of,course you did. Right...Let's move it along. I was saying ...'

Repeat Steps One, Two & Three for the remainder of your main ideas. Because you've done the first block carefully, the rest should come fairly easily.

4. How to Write a Speech: Step Four

Between each of your main ideas you need to provide a pathway. This links them for your listeners. The clearer the path, the easier it is for them to make the transition or move from one idea to the next. If your speech contains more than three main ideas and each is building on the last, then you may consider using a 'catch-up' or small summary as part of your transition.

Go back through your main ideas linking each of them. Try each transition or link out loud and listen to yourself. Write them down when you're satisfied they are as clear and concise as you can make them.

5. How to Write a Speech: Step Five: The Ending

The ending is what you leave with your audience. Ideally it is highly memorable as well as a quick summary of your main ideas. You want the ending to live on in the minds of your listeners so they continue to dwell on what you've said.

One of the worst mistakes you can make as a public speaker is talking too long. Not only will you send some folks to never, never land, you will make some of them downright mad. It doesn't matter if your entire speech was brilliant and the audience came away with information that will change their lives. If you talk too long, they will leave saying, "That speaker just wouldn't quit." Don't let this happen to you! Say what you have to say and sit down. Before you do, give them a well thought out closing.

The last thing you say may be the most remembered. You must put as much time into selecting and practising your closing as you put into any other part of your presentation. Just like your opening, your closing does not have to be humorous. It could be motivational, challenging, thoughtful, respectful of the length of the presentation, or it could restate your point in a different way. This ending segment will have a strong influence on what the audience takes home with them when you are done. Please, at sometime during your talk ask the audience to do something. If you haven't asked them to do something by now, the closing is your last chance.

If the subject is appropriate, humorous closings are effective. If you leave them laughing and applauding, you will exit, but an extremely positive impression about you will remain. Another good reason to leave them laughing is that the room will not be deadly silent as you are walking back to your seat. We all do love laughter and feeling good; finishing a speech humorously gives you and the audience an opportunity to feel great. Speeches that are for entertainment purposes only should generally leave the audience laughing.

Finally, if the subject is not appropriate to end with laughter, you could end with a touching story or quotation that leaves the audience thoughtful and quiet. Even the most serious public speaking subjects can benefit from humour, but the humour should be sprinkled throughout the body of the presentation. Don't put it at the end because closings are powerful and the audience will think your overall attitude toward the subject is flippant.

This same technique can be very effective in ending a mostly humorous speaking engagement. Have them laughing all along while you make your points. Then finish seriously. This contrast will create a great impact. It will convey the fact that you believe in a lighthearted approach to the subject, but the results are very serious to you.

Don't be afraid to use humour when you speak in public. Just make sure you learn to do it right.

This is also where you insert any call to action you might have for your speech.

Example: The desired outcome of a speech persuading people to vote for you in an upcoming election is that they do so. You can help that outcome along by calling them to register their support by signing a prepared pledge statement as they leave.

Example: The desired outcome is increased sales figures. The call to action is made urgent with the introduction of time specific incentives:

'You have three weeks from the time you leave this hall to make that dream family holiday in New Zealand yours. Can you do it? Will you do it? The kids will love it. Your wife will love it. Do it now!'

A clue for working out what the most appropriate call to action might be, is to go back to the original purpose for giving the speech.

a) What was it? Was it to motivate or inspire?
b) Was it to persuade to a particular point of view?
c) Was it to share specialist information?
d) Was it to celebrate a person, a place, time or event?

Ask yourself what you want people to do as a result of having listened to your speech.

Write your ending and test it out loud.

6. How to Write a Speech: Step Six

Once you've got the filling (main ideas) the linking and the ending in place, it's time to focus on the introduction.

The introduction comes last as it's the most important part of your speech. This is the bit that either has people sitting up alert or slumped and waiting for you to end (and that's tough if you've only just got to your feet and opened your mouth!).

What makes a great opening? You want one that makes listening to you the only thing the audience want to do. You want them to forget they're hungry or that their chair is hard or that the bills need paying.

The answer is to capture their interest straightaway. This is called the 'hook'. It's what you dangle in front of them to entice them to listen to you. Hooks come in as many forms as there are speeches and audiences. Your task is work out what the specific hook is to catch your audience. Go back to the purpose. Why are you giving this speech? Once you have your answer, consider your call to action. What do you want the audience to do as a result of listening to you? Next think about the imaginary or real person you wrote for when you were focusing on your main ideas.

Ask yourself, if I were him/her what would appeal?

a) Is it humour?
b) Would shock tactics work?
c) Is it formality or informality?
d) Is it an outline of what you're going to cover, including the call to action?
e) Or is it a mix of all these elements?

Here's an example from a fictional political speech. The speaker is lobbying for votes. His audience consists of predominately workers whose future's are not secure.

'How's your imagination? Good? Great, I'm glad. Because we're going to put it to work starting right now. I want you to see your future. What does it look like? Are you happy? Is everything as you want it to be? No? Let's change that. We could do it. And we could do it today. At the end of this speech you're going to be given the opportunity to change your world, for a better one....No, I'm not a magician or a simpleton with big ideas and precious little common sense. I'm an ordinary man, just like you.'

And then our speaker is off into his main points supported by examples. The end, which he has already foreshadowed in his opening, is the call to vote for him.

Experiment with several openings until you've found the one that serves your audience, subject matter and purpose best.

And that's it! Writing your speech is very nearly done. There's just one more step to go!

7. How to Write a Speech: Step Seven

On the first read through you are checking to make sure you've got your main points in their correct order with supporting material,l plus an effective opening and closing passage.

On the second read through you are checking the linking passages or transitions from point to point to make sure they are clear and easily followed.

On the third read through you are checking your sentence structure, language use and tone.

On the fourth read through you are making sure you've appealed to all your listeners.

Have you given them 'pictures' to see?

Is there enough 'action'?

Have you made them think with a variety of ideas?

Have you varied your sentence structure to make it interesting to listen to?

Is your language use inclusive or exclusive?

Once you've passed those checks, go through it once more. This time, read it aloud slowly and time yourself. If it's too long for the time allowance you've been given make the necessary cuts. A good place to start is by looking at your examples rather than the main ideas themselves. If you've used several to illustrate one, cut the least important out. Also look to see if you've repeated yourself unnecessarily or gone off track.

Hint: When you use a summary as part of a transition do not repeat all of the information for each point! Just use enough to remind your audience of the idea and move on. The downside of repeating everything is boring them! The same is true for unnecessary diversions. If it's not relevant, cut it out.

Repeat the process: condensing and tightening your information until you read through fits just under your time allowance.

And once you have finished how to write a speech, be ready for REHEARSAL!

5 Delivery and Presentation

Presentation and delivery are important aspects of a good speech. The following tips should be borne in mind while you make your presentation.

1. Show Your Passion

If there is one tip to give, it would be to be passionate about your topic and let that enthusiasm come out. Yes, you need great content. Yes, you need professional, well-designed visuals. But it is all for naught if you do not have a deep, heartfelt belief in your topic. The biggest item that separates mediocre presenters from world class ones is the ability to connect with an audience in an honest and exciting way. Don't hold back. Be confident. And let your passion for your topic come out for all to see.

2. Start Strong

You've heard it before: First impressions are powerful. Believe it. The first 2–3 minutes of the presentation are the most important. The audience wants to like you and they will give you a few minutes at the beginning to engage them—don't miss the opportunity. Most presenters fail here because they ramble on too long about superfluous background information or their personal/professional history, etc.

3. Keep It Short

Humans have short attention spans when it comes to passively sitting and listening to a speaker. Audience attention is greatest at the opening and then again when you say something like "In conclusion...." This is just the human condition, especially so for the busy (often tired) knowledge worker of today. So, if you have 30 minutes for your talk, finish in 25 minutes. It is better to have the audience wanting more (of you) than to feel that they have had more than enough. Professional entertainers know this very well.

4. Move Away from the Podium

Get closer to your audience by moving away from or in front of the podium. The podium is a barrier between you and the audience, but the goal of our presentation is to connect with the audience. Removing physical barriers between you and the audience will help you build a rapport and make a connection.

5. Use a Remote Control Device

To advance your slides and builds, use a small, handheld remote. A handheld remote will allow you to move away from the podium. This is an absolute must.

6. Remember the "B" Key

If you press the "B" key while your PowerPoint or Keynote slide is showing, the screen will go blank. This is useful if you need to digress or move off the topic presented on the slide. By having the slide blank, all the attention can now be placed back on you. When you are ready to move on, just press the "B" key again and the image reappears.

7. Make Good Eye Contact

Try looking at individuals rather than scanning the group. Since you are using a computer, you never need to look at the screen behind you—just glance down at the computer screen briefly. One sure way to lose an audience is to turn your back on them. And while you're maintaining great eye contact, don't forget to smile as well. Unless your topic is very grim, a smile can be a very powerful thing.

8. Keep the Lights on

If you are speaking in a meeting room or a classroom, the temptation is to turn the lights off so that the slides look better. But go for a compromise between a bright screen image and ambient room lighting. Turning the lights off—besides inducing sleep—puts all the focus on the screen. The audience should be looking at you more than the screen. Today's projectors are bright enough to allow you to keep many of the lights on.

9. Use a TV for Small Groups

If you are presenting to a small group, then you can connect your computer to a large TV. With a TV screen, you can keep all or most of the lights on. Make sure your text and graphics are large enough to be seen on the small screen. You will probably have to increase the type size significantly

10. At All Times be Courteous, Gracious, Professional

When audience members ask questions or give comments, you should be gracious and thank them for their input. Even if someone is being difficult, you must keep to the high ground and at all times be a gentleman or lady and courteously deal with such individuals. The true professional can always remain cool and in control. Remember, it is your reputation, so always remain gracious even with the most challenging of audiences.

A few helpful tips will

Controlling Nerves

Most speakers feel that "butterflies in the stomach" nervous feeling as they anticipate and deliver a speech. The good news is that good practice and experience often minimises nervousness for public speaking. There are also some helpful tips to decrease the effects of nervous stage fright:

1. To prevent unnecessary stress, arrive early and ensure your audiovisual aids are in working order.
2. Eating too much before a presentation can make you sluggish.
3. Drinking too much coffee or caffeinated beverages can increase your jitters.
4. Practise, practise, practise, and you will look more comfortable and natural because you will be familiar with the content. The more prepared you are, the less you have to be nervous about.
5. At least 30 minutes before your presentation, go to a calm environment and focus on the presentation at hand.

Speaking Confidentlly

It's essential to start your presentation strongly and confidently. A strong introduction can build rapport and credibility as you quickly gain an audience's trust and interest. Begin by establishing good eye contact throughout the room and try to create a connection with your entire audience. If it helps you get going, focus on a few people in the audience who appear interested in order to gain your confidence.

If you're unconfident, usually the audience will not know. It is possible to appear confident by maintaining eye contact, an open body posture, and a relaxed yet professional demeanor. A few points need to be remembered:

1. Emphasize important points by pausing for a few seconds after you deliver them.
2. Speak slowly and don't mumble.
3. Don't end each sentence with a rising inflection (like asking questions).
4. Don't let your voice trail off at the end of each sentence.

5. Try your best to be conversational and not reliant on your notes.
6. Minimise distracting behaviour and instead strive to be natural.

Concluding a Speech Effectively

It's likely that of all the points made in your speech, the audience will remember the beginning and the end of your speech the best. Therefore, your conclusion must be strong.

To close effectively, you should give the audience a signal that you are nearing the end and then reiterate your main points. Your audience will increase their attention as you notify them that your presentation is coming to an end. End with a nice, succinct sentence or two. This is much more powerful and effective than a long, drawn out conclusion. You don't want your audience to wish your presentation would end soon!

A few points must be borne in mind.

1. Don't act like you want to leave as soon as you possibly can.
2. Keep a close eye on your time and try your best to stay within the time limits.
3. If time runs short, don't rush through all your remaining slides. It's okay to end your presentation short with a strong conclusion and then if time allows, return to some of your skipped slides.
4. Minimise distracting behaviour and instead strive to be natural.

Handling Questions during a Speech

After a strong speech, a difficult time can be the question and answer session afterward. The uncertainty can be challenging, as your presentation can go in many different directions. It's important to maintain a confident appearance and stay in control during this time.

Good preparation is the key for handling questions. As you prepare your speech, try to look at it from different angles and perspectives in order to identify any gaps or potential questions your audience might ask. Even better, practise your speech in front of a real audience and get them to ask as many questions as possible.

If a questioner is hostile or aggressive, you need to maintain a gracious and polite demeanour. Request to talk to the person individually after the presentation, or deflect the question to the general audience. If a question is irrelevant or off-topic, you need to carefully steer the question back to your speech.

A few important points to remember are:

1. Don't become defensive or argumentative.
2. Always think carefully before giving a response. Ask for more details if a question is unclear.
3. Compliment good questions to help encourage your audience.
4. For particularly challenging questions, you can sometimes buy extra time by getting some water or referring to your notes.

Effective Delivery

For years two guidelines for effective delivery have been naturalness and poise. A speaker's delivery should not draw attention from the content of the message—as it might, for example, if it were overly dramatic or reflected lack of confidence. Good delivery involves much more than mere fluency in speaking. It includes the effective use of many visual and vocal cues: eye contact, hand gestures, posture, and general physical appearance as well as vocal quality, pitch, volume, and rate of speech."

Delivering Your Speech

Scripts, Notes or Memory?

It's now time to prepare to deliver your speech. If you are nervous or inexperienced, you will probably want to choose to read your speech from a script or from notes.

Reading From a Script: Reading your entire speech from a script may give you confidence and ensure that nothing is forgotten or omitted; however it is the least desirable option for delivering your speech. You will find it more difficult to see your audience, and make it harder for them to get involved with you. When reading from a script it is extremely difficult to have eye contact with your audience.

Using Notes: If you are not confident enough to recite your speech from memory, then the use of notes is a much more desirable option than using a complete script. Your notes should consist of the keywords or points of your speech—a skeleton of thoughts or words around which you can build your speech. You may refer to your notes occasionally to maintain the thread of your speech, while for the most part of you will be able to speak directly to the audience.

Reciting From Memory: You may prefer to recite from memory. However you should only do this if you are comfortable speaking publicly, and not prone to loss of concentration (or memory!). As with reading from a script, you should be careful not to lapse into a monotonous recitation of your speech.

Speech Delivery Tips

1. Make sure that your appearance is well presented.
2. Speak clearly, and adjust your voice so that everyone can hear you. Don't shout for the sake of being loud.
3. It is common to speak rapidly when nervous, try to take your time speaking.

4. Effectively used, a pause in your speech can be used to emphasise a point, or to allow the audience to react to a fact, anecdote or joke.
5. Make eye contact with your audience. This helps to build trust and a relationship between the speaker and the listeners.
6. Do not fidget or make other nervous gestures with your hands. Do not keep your hands in your pockets. Do use hand gestures effectively.
7. Be yourself, allow your own personality to come across in your speech

Presentation and Storyteller's Promises

Before Anything

What is the purpose of your piece? Are you presenting details? Are you giving product information? Do you have to convince anyone of anything?

Titles Matter

Give up "clever". Go instead for short, impactful titles.

Load the Front

Your audience will form a "value" opinion on your presentation fairly quickly. Give them a big start, with a lot of enthusiasm for your topic. Don't "phone it in".

Explicit Promises

The agenda, whether on a slide or verbally, is where people "seat" themselves mentally for your presentation. If you give them three points, you'll cover. Make sure you hit them.

This is LIVE

Take advantage of that fact. You can adjust to the audience. You can pep them up if they're lagging. You can give them a break if they are looking lost.

Keep it Tight

Nothing kills any presentation like tangents. If you're talking about a particular topic, don't talk about another topic which may not be relevant to your speech. Sidebar comments are also disruptive. Stay on target.

Finish Strong

Lots of people's presentations just seem to end. They go, "That's it," and they wait for the applause they expect. Let's go into that further. Finish strong. By the end of your presentation, people should be nodding their head vigorously. They might be affirming your data presentation. They might be agreeing with the point you so masterfully made. But you should be looking out on a sea of nodding heads. Often, this isn't the way presentations end. Presenters, especially nervous ones, have expended a lot of emotional energy to get to this point. They are feeling exhausted mentally from keeping everything straight in their heads, and from reacting to the audience. You can't stop now. Give them a strong finish. If you've hit them with lots of product details, here's a great chance to tell them the one most important emotional or story-based thing you want them to remember. Because most of the facts are seeping out of their ears, tell them: "When my grandmother first logged on and downloaded a video of my daughter, she cried. No, not because the kid is so cute. She said, 'I'm on the internet.' " Believe me, that image will far surpass the product that you are trying to promote. You are the Authority. As a presenter, you are a storyteller. You have them mesmerised. You are the one standing before the fire while others watch. They trust you explicitly and implicitly to use their time well, but also to entertain them. Believe me, if you betray that trust, the fire's not that far away.

The Moment of Truth

Gulp. So you are sitting there, about to be introduced. Now what?

Take several deep breaths as you are being introduced (but don't sigh!). Visualise your rehearsed opening statement; don't improvise at the last moment.

State your objectives at start of your talk, then restate them again at the end of the talk. In between, discuss how your material relates to these objectives.

Unless you intentionally have had experience as a stand-up comic, avoid making jokes. The results can be disappointing, and may suggest an unprofessional attitude.

Choose a natural, moderate rate of speech and use automatic, moderate gestures.

Monitor your behavior, and avoid habitual behaviours (pacing, fumbling change in pocket, twirling hair).

Laser pointers are wonderful pointing devices, but remember not to point them at the audience. They are best used by flashing the pointer on and off, so that the place you are indicating is illuminated briefly. Don't swirl the laser around and around one place on the projection screen, or sweep it from place to place across the screen. This is very distracting for the audience, and they will end up watching the pointer and not listening to what you are saying.

Likewise, and for the same reasons, avoid using the cursor as in pointer in your computer presentations.

Also try to avoid pointing things out on the computer's monitor at the podium; although the presenter's natural tendency is to concentrate on the monitor's screen, the audience will be looking over your shoulder at the projection screen and won't be able to see where your finger is pointing. If you find yourself doing this, power-off or disable the monitor to force yourself to concentrate on the projection screen!

Enthusiasm for your topic is contagious, but don't overdo it—you'll alienate the audience.

Converse with your audience. Involve them in the process of the presentation by posing questions and making eye contact. Be patient if you ask a question—answers sometimes take time to formulate.

Keep an eye on your time, and don't run over your limit. Ever.

Be prepared for interruptions (late arrivals, cell phones or pagers, burned out projector bulbs, fire drills, etc.).

If you must turn down the room lights, don't turn them off entirely. Don't leave the lights down any longer than necessary — remember to turn them back up! Of course, the snores from the sleeping audience may remind you to turn the lights back on if you've forgotten.

Don't apologise for any aspect of your presentation. This should be your very best effort; if you have to apologise, you haven't done your job properly.

Don't criticise aspects of the trip, city, facilities, etc. during your talk. This is another way to alienate your audience quickly. For instance, they may or may not have chosen to live in this horrible climate, but it isn't your place to remind them how horrible it is. Remember that you are a guest and it is impolite to exhibit your prejudices publicly.

Strive to have a prepared and memorable summary. If nothing else, the take home message is what the audience will remember after you leave.

When you reach the summary and are about to finish, resist the temptation to add a few last impromptu words. They will be unpractised, and will be the last thing many of your audience will hear you say. End your talk with the insightful, firm summary statement you have prepared.

Don't be afraid to give yourself credit for your own work, but do remember to give others credit where due. One prefer to do this early, others may prefer doing it later in the talk. If planned for later in the talk, don't forget to acknowledge these people's efforts, even if you have to skip a statement or two to remain within your time frame. The best friend of one of these contributors may be in your audience!

If you include slides borrowed from other people, or slides which include other people's data or figures, always give credit to these people right on that slide. This shows a professional attitude, and (better yet) can save you many words of explanation.

How to Rehearse

Many people say they don't know how to rehearse. Many others ask why they should. They think once they've written the speech it's ready for delivery. What they don't realise is rehearsing can make an ordinary speech extraordinary!

Think about it. Writing is only part of the process. It's delivery that completes it.

If you've sat through ho-hum presentations finding your finger nails more interesting, the odds are the delivery was less than polished. The content may have been excellent. It may have been well researched but because the speaker lacked the basic delivery skills, the entire speech was compromised. That is why you need to know how to rehearse.

How you deliver makes the difference. This is how you reach and communicate with your audience. You owe it to them and yourself to communicate with confidence!

Get ready to be extraordinary now. Before you begin learning how to rehearse it's time to make a critical decision. What you decide will have an impact on how you rehearse and deliver your speech.

Make a choice between reading your speech from a word-for-word script (this is where you have EVERYTHING you are going to say fully written out) or using cue cards on which you have written the headings of your main ideas in order and the key words associated with each of them. (Cue cards are easily made from small index cards. They are numbered to keep them ordered. Generally one card is used per main idea. The key words and phrases are clearly written on each. You speak covering each topic and the transitions between them from memory.)

If you are committing your entire speech to memory, then you need have neither cue cards nor a script.

There are positives and negatives for all three options.

Word-for-word Script

Using a full word-for-word script can be positive as it acts as a safety net for a nervous or first-time speaker. The downside is reading.

When people read they tend not to be making eye contact with their audience. And neither is their voice being projected out to reach them. Instead it's focused downward toward the page. If the script is in their hands, then they're not free for gestures and there is always the temptation to mask or cover their face with it. If a stand is used to place papers on, then it's between them and the audience, creating a barrier.

There are ways around it.

The first is to place the stand to one side instead of directly in front.

The second is make sure the stand is at your eye-level height to ensure easy upright reading. (You won't be bending down and therefore presenting the top of your head rather than your face to the audience.)

Another is to make sure the script is easily read. (A mess of scribbled notes doesn't cut it! If you lose your place, you'll be struggling to find it. So type it up in a clear good sized easy to read font, double space and number your pages before printing out.)

If full scripting is your choice, make a clear, clean copy of your speech.

Cue Cards

The positives for using cue cards are smaller than a full size script and therefore can be held unobtrusively in one hand. Because you are not using a stand, you're not blocked off from your audience. This means you are free to meet them. You can use a lot of eye contact and direct your speech where you wish. And because you're not following a word-for-word script, you're freer to be more spontaneous.

The downside of cue cards is apparent if they haven't been prepared properly. They won't be in order and therefore you run the risk of getting muddled. If they're not clear and easily read, you run the same risk. The other major negative is what happens if you stumble in remembering how you linked your ideas together.

If cue cards are your choice, you'll need to prepare them before you go on to How to Rehearse.

This is how you prepare good cue cards: Get a pack of small index cards from your stationer or cut clean pieces of cardboard to a size that fits comfortably in your palm.

Go through your speech notes and take the MAIN IDEA HEADINGS from each section. Only write down enough to jog your memory. If you have specific names of people, places or processes to remember be sure to include them.

Make sure you space your notes on your cards and write clearly. Another useful tip is to colour code with a highlighter separating Main Ideas, Examples and Links.

A Main Idea Heading might be orange, the examples blue and all your links, green. The benefit is your eyes will find them more quickly if you have to search for them.

Number each card to keep them in the correct sequence.

Do not be tempted to try and write your entire speech out in very little writing! It will set you up for difficulties.

Prepare and practise with one card to get your system fail-proof before you do the whole of your speech.

Once you have the full set completed, make a hole in the top left hand corner of each of the cards. Thread through a piece of string long enough to make a loop and knot it securely. This will keep your cards together and enable you to flip them easily. (Saves a lot of embarrassment if you drop them!).

Memorising Your Speech

The positives for committing your speech entirely to memory is that you meet the audience completely free of notes. You can gesture when necessary, provided of course, that you can keep yourself on track.

While this option is good for speakers used to being in front of people, it can be daunting for a novice. It is also difficult to pull off with certain styles of speech. For example, if you are giving a complex business presentation which includes the breakdown and analysis of large chunks of data, this would be risky. So think carefully and wisely before making the decision to go solo. Styles of speech most suitable are eulogies, wedding, retirement speeches...the type which includes personal storytelling. Here it can work brilliantly although you do need to keep in mind over-learning can make delivery wooden.

Tips on How to Rehearse

Aim to have at least three rehearsals before delivering your speech in front of an audience.

The first two rehearsals are to iron out any glitches in either your text or delivery and to integrate any resource material you may be using. These could be photographs, a power point presentation, etc.

The third is a dress rehearsal for the real thing.

1. Start by either saying (if memorised)/reading your notes or using your cue cards to run through several times out loud. This is to familiarise yourself with the flow. Do not worry about expression or gesture right now. Your focus is on getting the flow fluid!

2. Now practise in front of a mirror or a video camera. This time the focus on delivery.

   Take note of habitual unconscious gestures like fiddling with your hair, pulling faces when you can't remember what is next, standing awkwardly, pulling at your clothes, irregular breathing, running you out of breath over long sentences or holding your breath which weakens your voice making it sound strained, etc., and try to avoid them consciously.

   Avoid racing your speech through, and having pauses or breaks in the wrong places.

   Practise saying repeatedly specific words or phrases that trip you up.

   Make sure that you don't hold your notes in a way that masks your face.Avoid rustling or fiddling with your notes if you are reading from them.

   Don't dropping or raise your voice at the end of sentences. Be very sure that you don't mumble, but are clear and loud enough to be heard.

   Avoid using repeated phrases, e.g., 'and then I...', 'and then I...', 'and then I...'

   Be sure that you don't indulge in repeated fillers like 'um', 'er', etc.

   Be conscious of your gestures, whether there is lack of gesture or too much gesture.

   Make sure you have eye contact with your audience and that there is a nice smile on your face.

Ensure that there is minimal variation in tone or pace.

Be methodical in the use of resources by having them in order of presentation, etc.

3. When you catch yourself doing any of the grievous crimes mentioned above, STOP.

   Take a deep breath, fix the problem and start again from where you left off.

4. If it's a matter of when and where to pause either for a breath or to stress an important point, mark it on your cue cards or script. In the same way mark passages needing to taken more slowly, or words requiring emphasis.
5. Remember if you have included a joke, they need special timing attention. Point up the cue for the audience to laugh by briefly holding back the punch line. Leave space for the audience to respond before carrying on. If it bombs and nobody laughs, keep going as if nothing had happened!
6. Run through your entire presentation as though it was the real thing.

Wear the clothes you'll be wearing for the event so you can be sure you feel comfortable and that they're not restricting in any way.

Set up your stand if you are using one in a similar position to the one you'll use on the day.

If you are using any electronic equipment, for example, a microphone, be sure to rehearse with it.

If you can present to a friend or a member of your family, do it! Their feedback could provide invaluable last minute suggestions. Tell them exactly what you want feedback on before you start. Ask them to take notes during your speech to give to you after it's finished.

Do not STOP if you falter. Keep going.

When you're done, make any minor adjustments you need to and then YOU ARE READY.

Remember to ENJOY yourself!

How to Deal with a Hostile Audience

1. Listen carefully to the question and repeat it aloud. Make sure you understood the question correctly and that your audience knows the question to which you are responding.
2. Answer directly. Look directly at the person asking the question. Give simple answers to simple questions. If the question demands a lengthy reply, agree to discuss it later with anyone interested.
3. Refer to your speech. Whenever possible, tie your answer to a point in your speech. Look upon these questions as a way to reinforce and clarify your presentation.
4. Anticipate areas of questioning. Prepare factual support material in three or four areas in which you anticipate questions.
5. Be friendly, always keep your temper. A cool presentation creates an aura of confidence. When the questioner is hostile respond as if he or she were a friend. Any attempt to "put down" your questioner with sarcasm will immediately draw the audience's sympathy to the questioner.
6. Always tell the truth. If you try to bend the truth, you almost always will be caught. Play it straight, even if your position is momentarily weakened.
7. Treat two questions from the same person as two separate questions.
8. Don't place your hands on your hips or point at the audience. These are scolding poses and give you the appearance of preaching.

9. Keep things moving. There is a rhythm to a good question-and-answer exchange. They volley back and forth in a brisk manner. Keep your answers brief and to the point with many members of the audience participating.
10. Conclude smartly. Be prepared with some appropriate closing remarks. End with a summary statement that wraps up the essential message you want them to remember.

How to Use Props

Learning how to use props effectively is one of the best gifts you can give yourself as a speaker. You want to make your presentation the best you can. You want it to 'zing'. And that's just what getting to know how to use props will do for you.

Think of it this way. Which of these alternatives is more effective? Would you rather hear about a holiday in Mexico? Or would you rather hear about the holiday and see a few carefully chosen photographs and a sombrero?

Here's one more example. Try explaining something like the current weather patterns, or the fluctuation of the US dollar over the past year without using either diagrams or graphs. It's tough. It's not impossible but it is definitely a challenge.

When you learn how to use props as part of your speech, you are giving your audience so much more. They add value.

The main benefits of learning how to use props are:

1. *Clarity:* You reduce the number of words you have to use to explain a concept or event. Remember that old saying, 'A picture is worth a thousand words'? Now think what a well-drawn graph or diagram does. Or what an aptly chosen photograph does to show a current event. The Hurrcane Katrina pictures are an effective example. The devastation

and misery wrought by the winds and flooding didn't need words. We saw and in seeing, felt it.

2. *Credibility:* You become more believable through your audience seeing something to reinforce your words. Another old saying says it for us like this: 'Seeing is believing'. When we add 'show' to 'tell' our credibility rating soars.

Does this mean every speech needs props to make it more effective? The short answer is, No. The longer answer is to consider carefully the nature of the speech you're preparing and its content.

Ask yourself: What could I show (or demonstrate) that would add value for my audience? Obviously, your answers will vary hugely. Do add any time or financial constraints into your decision making process. It takes time to prepare props to use effectively. It may take money as well. Weigh up the pros and cons before going ahead. If you don't have time, simplify your plans. It is better to have a few simple well-presented props than a grand incomplete scheme. You may even decide that this time, props are not for you.

What Can I Use as a Prop?

Absolutely anything at all!

However before you get too excited consider:

1. Whether or not your intended prop fits your topic. Something brought along merely because it is interesting or a novelty needs to be left at home. Props should not divert from the purpose or scope of your speech. If they do, they are irrelevant and could undermine your credibility as a speaker.
2. The suitability of the prop for your audience. Think carefully before showing shocking photographs or any material that may offend even if it fits within the theme of your speech.

3. The monetary value of the prop. Some things are too valuable to shift around without making the necessary arrangements with your insurance company. If you are willing to do that, good. If not, perhaps photographs or videotape will suffice.
4. The emotional value of the prop. Are you willing to take responsibility for having very special items on show?
5. The suitability of your prop to the venue you are using. For example: If it's a huge hall, will your small collection of miniatures actually be seen when you hold them up? Think about the setting before committing yourself to a particular prop and shaping your speech around its use. In this example close-up photos might be better than the real things.

Given below are tips on how to use props.

1. The best way is to integrate them into the body of your speech. It is more effective to show and tell as you go, rather than wait to the end of your speech and then show. By then your audience may have forgotten why it is they are looking at your graph, photograph or grandmother clock!
2. Use clear descriptions of each item you use. Give enough information to satisfy interest without going on too long. You do not want to stop the flow of your speech by dwelling on one aspect.
3. Less IS more. Choose the BEST examples of whatever you've got to show. Less is more effective. Don't clutter an audience's minds with too many to take in.
4. Test before committing yourself to their use. Be sure the prop works in the venue. For example: If it's big, can it fit through the door, or on the stage?
5. If you're using any electronic equipment to show photographs, graphs, etc., test it beforehand. Leave yourself

enough time to familiarise yourself with how to operate it properly or to fix any problems you may find.

6. If you're reliant on someone else to operate equipment, be sure to rehearse fully with them. Give clear instructions about precisely what you want done, when. Have all your material in the right order ready for them. Prepare a 'cue sheet' for them to follow.
7. If you have a range of props to use throughout your speech, put them in order. Label them if necessary. Arrange them so they are easily picked up, put down and not in either your or your audience's way.
8. If you are demonstrating as well as showing, test and retest to make sure what you are doing is effective.

What's the difference? Demonstrating is active. You are doing something. Showing is passive. You are holding something up to be looked at.

Example:

'Here's a remarkably easy drawing technique. I start here...' And the speaker does it on a drawing board in such a way to be visible to the audience.

'Here's the result of a drawing exercise...' And the speaker holds up his drawing pad to display the completed exercise.

The first is active and the second is passive.

NB. When you demonstrate, the key is simplicity. Keep everything you do to a minimum. Think of how a live cooking demonstration is shown on television. Every aspect is prepared beforehand. The movements of the cook are clear and they've rehearsed their speech to fit precisely what they're doing so the audience can follow easily.

9. Sometimes our props need other people to demonstrate them. If that's the case for you, those people need to be part of your rehearsal process. They need to know what you're going to say, how you want them to react, where you want

them to be on the stage (or wherever you're presenting), when you want them to come on and when to leave. And if you're going to have children taking part, make doubly sure they know what they're doing! Kids on stage with you can be great fun but the reverse is true too. It's up to you to make them feel at ease and confident about what you've asked them to do. Make it safe for them as well as yourself.

In summary, learning how to use props well will enhance how the audience receives your speech. It can give it the 'zing' factor.

6 General Tips for Effective Speech

"Half the world is composed of people who have something to say and can't; the other half have nothing to say and keep saying it."

Planning and preparing an informative speech can be intimidating, especially if you're relatively new to formal public speaking.

Anyone can give a speech. Not everyone can give an effective speech. To give an effective speech there are six elements you should consider.

1. Be prepared. Being prepared is by far the most important element. How many times do you practise your speech? As a general rule, you should spend about 30 hours of preparation and rehearsal time for every hour you will be speaking. Use a tape recorder or videotape yourself. This will help you to get an accurate picture of how you speak.
2. Give of yourself. Use personal examples and stories in your speech to you're your point whenever possible. Make sure your stories help to emphasize or support your point. The stories must match your message. In either case be willing to give of yourself by sharing some of yourself with the audience.
3. Stay relaxed. To stay relaxed you should be prepared. Also, focus on your message and not the audience. Use gestures, including walking patterns. Practise the opening of your

speech and plan exactly how you will say it. The audience will judge you in the first 30 seconds they see you.

4. Use natural humour. Don't try to be a stand-up comedian. Use natural humour by poking fun at yourself and something you said or did. Be sure NOT to make fun of anyone in the audience. People will laugh with you when you poke fun at yourself but don't overdo it.
5. Plan your body and hand positions. During the practice of your speech look for occasions where you can use a gesture. Establish three positions where you will stand and practise not only how to move to them but where in your speech do you move. Pick three positions, one on centre stage, one to your right, and one to your left. Do not hide behind the lectern. When you do move maintain eye contact with the audience.
6. Pay attention to all details. Make sure you have the right location (school, hotel, room and time). Make sure you know how to get to where you are speaking. Ask how large an audience you will be speaking to. Make sure you bring all your visual aids and plenty of handouts. Arrive early so you can check out where you will be speaking and make any last minute adjustments.
7. Having confidence in your presentation. Believe in yourself. You've done a great job preparing. Have confidence that you are an expert in your subject matter! As many athletes know, envisioning yourself being successful more than often leads you to become successful.
8. Have a positive self-image. Think positive! Envision yourself being successful. The mental battle is just as important as any other.

The audience will also hope that you do well, as they want to watch a good presentation and benefit from the time spent. They are not the enemy. They're supportive of you!

Appropriate Body Image for Speeches

What can make or break a good speech are the non-verbal cues that you send to your audience. Even before you speak one word, audience members have most likely already formed judgements about you based on your appearance and body language. Practise your speech in front of a mirror and watch your body, face, and clothes carefully. What are your hands, posture, and facial expressions conveying to your audience?

Evaluate your posture and body image

1. Is your head up high?
2. Is your posture straight and upright?
3. Are your hands relaxed?
4. Is your body blocking your audio-visual aids?

Avoid bad habits

1. Don't lean backward or slouch. This can suggest a negative, disinterested attitude.
2. Don't cross your legs.
3. Avoid placing your hands in your pockets.
4. Don't chew gum. The chewing motion can be distracting.

Face and facial expressions

1. Are you making eye contact with your audience?
2. Are your facial muscles relaxed?
3. Are you smiling comfortably?
4. Be sure your hair does not get into your face.

Dressing appropriately

1. Carry a comb, hairbrush, travel iron, and clothes brush, to ensure your appearance looks good.
2. Tuck in your shirt.

3. Be sure your clothes are pressed and clean, and your shoes polished.
4. Avoid wearing anything too flashy or distracting. You want your audience thinking about your ideas, not your clothes.

Improving Your Voice for Speeches

The projection of your voice and the tone of your speech can make a critical difference on your presentation. Some novice speakers breathe too quickly or speak too quickly or quietly, leading to a less effective presentation.

Project your voice out into the room. The more you practise this, your vocal cords will strengthen and it will get easier over time.

Some of the following tips may be useful to you.

1. Practise breathing deeply and slowly.
2. Listen to yourself project a few lines of your speech.
3. Carry a water bottle for your throat if it becomes dry.
4. Lozenges, candy, lemons, and honey are foods that some people swear by. Experiment and see what works for you.

Reducing Tension Before Speeches

Your body naturally becomes tense when you get ready to give a speech. This tension can cause you to speak too quickly, make you fidgety, or otherwise behave unnaturally. At one point, some people surveyed said that they would rather die than give a speech! Fortunately, there are exercises you can do to reduce the tension that comes with “stage fright”.

Here are some easy-to-do exercises to reduce tension:

Hand squeeze

1. Make a fist with your left hand.

2. Wrap the fist with your right hand.
3. Squeeze the fist tightly for three seconds and hold.
4. Switch to the other hand and repeat.

Arm and shoulder stretch

1. Slowly extend your arms as wide as possible.
2. Hold for three seconds.
3. Slowly make ten small circles with your arms.
4. Slowly make ten medium circles with your arms.
5. Slowly make ten large circles with your arms.
6. Reverse directions and repeat.

Real speech preparation means digging something out of your self. You have to gather facts and arrange your thoughts. As you collect the ideas, you have to nurture your ideas and think about a unique way to express them in an organised manner.

A speech needs time to grow. Prepare for weeks, sleep on it, dream about it and let your ideas sink into your subconscious. Ask yourself questions, write down your thoughts, and keep adding new ideas. As you prepare every speech ask yourself the following questions.

1. In one concise sentence, what is the purpose of this speech?
2. Who is the audience? What is their main interest in this topic?
3. What do I really know and believe about this topic as it relates to this audience?
4. What additional research can I do?
5. What are the main points of this presentation?
6. What supporting information and stories can I use to support each of my main points?
7. What visual aids, if any, do I need?

8. Do I have an effective opening grabber?
9. In my final summary, how will I plan to tell them "What's In It For Me?"
10. Have I polished and prepared the language and words I will use?
11. Have I prepared a written and concise introduction for myself?
12. Have I taken care of the little details that will help me speak more confidently?

Body Language

Dr. Ralph C. Smeadly, the founder of Toastmasters International, wrote, "The speaker who stands and talks at ease is the one who can be heard without weariness. If his posture and gestures are so graceful and unobtrusive, that no one notices them, he may be counted as truly successful."

When your actions are wedded to your words, the impact of your speech will be strengthened. If your platform behaviour includes mannerisms unrelated to your spoken message, those actions will call attention to themselves and away from your speech. Below are provided five ways you can rid yourself of your distracting mannerisms.

1. Rid Yourself of Distracting Mannerisms

Eliminate vocal and visual impediments.

Some common faults of inexperienced or in-effective speakers are:

Gripping or leaning on the lectern, Finger tapping, Lip biting or licking, Toying with coins or jewellery, Frowning, Adjusting hair or clothing, Head wagging.

These have two things in common:

1. They are physical manifestations of simple nervousness.
2. They are performed unconsciously.

When you make a verbal mistake, you can easily correct it, because you can hear your own words, but you can't see yourself, so most distracting mannerisms go uncorrected. You can't eliminate them unless you know they exist.

Videotape yourself.

The first step in eliminating any superfluous behavior is to obtain an accurate perception of your body's image. This should include:

a) Posture
b) Gestures
c) Body movement
d) Facial expressions
e) Eye contact

The next step is to free yourself of physical behaviours that do not add to your speech. This can be accomplished by simply becoming aware of your problem areas. After you have videotaped yourself speaking, review the tape several times and make a list of all the distracting mannerisms you notice.

First review. Review your tape the first time without looking for mannerisms. Just listen to the presentation as if you were hearing it for the first time and evaluate the overall impact you experience from watching the tape.

Second review. Review your tape a second time (with the volume turned down) and look for visual distractions. Take notes on what you observe.

Third review. During this review, have the picture turned off and listen only to your voice. Many people have never even heard a taping of their own voice before. Become accustomed to listening to your voice. Get to know it as others hear it. Note what you like and what you don't like. Pay attention to the speed, the volume, and the tone of your voice.

Fourth review. Once you have made lists of both your distracting mannerisms and your more positive points, you are ready to have one or two family members watch the tape with you. Get their initial impression. Ask them to be honest.

Once you have completed these reviews, go over the list of all the distracting mannerisms you saw and heard. The next time you are having a conversation with someone you know well, try to notice whether you use any of these distracting mannerisms even in casual circumstances. Tackle each of your negative points one at a time.

2. *Build Self-confidence by Being Yourself*

The most important rule for making your body communicate effectively is to be yourself. The emphasis should be on the sharing of ideas, not on the performance.

Strive to be as genuine and natural as you are when you speak to family members and friends.

Many people say, "I'm okay in a small group, but when I get in front of a larger group I freeze." The only difference between speaking to a small informal group and to a sizable audience is the number of listeners. To compensate for this, you need only to amplify your natural behaviour. Be authentically yourself, but amplify your movements and expressions just enough so that the audience can see them.

3. *Let Your Body Mirror Your Feelings*

If you are interested in your subject, truly believe what you are saying, and want to share your message with others, your physical movements will come from within you and will be appropriate to what you are saying.

By involving yourself in your message, you'll be natural and spontaneous without having to consciously think about what you are doing or saying. For many of us, this isn't as easy as it sounds because it requires us to drop the mask that shields the "real self" in public.

To become an effective speaker, it is essential that you get rid of your mask and share your true feelings with your audience. Your audience wants to know how you feel about your subject. If you want to convince others, you must convey your convictions.

Speak from the heart and to the soul.

4. Build Self-confidence through Preparation

Nothing influences a speaker's mental attitude more than the knowledge that he or she is thoroughly prepared. This knowledge leads to self-confidence, which is a vital ingredient of effective public speaking.

How many of us have ever experienced a situation in which we had not prepared well for a presentation? How did we come across? On the other hand, think of those presentations that did go well. These are the ones that we had properly prepared for.

5. Use Your Everyday Speaking Situations

Whenever you speak to people, make an extra effort to notice how you speak. Observe, too, whether the facial expressions of your listeners indicate they do or do not understand what you are saying. Before calling to request something on the phone, plan and practise what you are going to say. Even this is essentially a short presentation. Another exercise is to prepare a 90-second presentation about yourself. Describe who you are and what you do. Record your presentation and review it using the four steps described above.

Since you are talking about yourself, you don't need to research the topic; however, you do need to prepare what you are going to say and how you are going to say it. Plan everything including your gestures and walking patterns.

Facial Expressions

Leave that deadpan expression to poker players. A speaker realises that appropriate facial expressions are an important part of effective communication. In fact, facial expressions are often the key determinant of the meaning behind the message. People watch a speaker's face during a presentation. When you speak, your face, more clearly than any other part of your body, communicates to others your attitudes, feelings and emotions.

Remove expressions that don't belong on your face.

Inappropriate expressions include distracting mannerisms or unconscious expressions not rooted in your feelings, attitudes and emotions. In much the same way that some speakers perform random, distracting gestures and body movements, nervous speakers often release excess energy and tension by unconsciously moving their facial muscles (e.g., licking lips, tightening the jaw).

One type of unconscious facial movement that is less apt to be read clearly by an audience is involuntary frowning. This type of frowning occurs when a speaker attempts to deliver a memorised speech. There are no rules governing the use of specific expressions. If you relax your inhibitions and allow yourself to respond naturally to your thoughts, attitudes and emotions, your facial expressions will be appropriate and will project sincerity, conviction, and credibility.

Eye Contact

Eye contact is the cement that binds together speakers and their audiences. When you speak, your eyes involve your listeners in your presentation. There is no surer way to break a communication bond between you and the audience than by failing to look at your listeners. No matter how large your audience may be, each listener wants to feel that you are talking to him or her.

The adage, "The eyes are the mirror of the soul," underlines the need for you to convince people with your eyes, as well as your words. Only by looking at your listeners as individuals can you convince them that you are sincere and are interested in them, and that you care whether they accept your message. When you speak, your eyes also function as a control device you can use to assure your listeners' attentiveness and concentration.

Eye contact can also help you to overcome nervousness by making your audience a known quantity. Effective eye contact is an important feedback device that makes the speaking situation a two-way communication process. By looking at your audience, you can determine how they are reacting. When you develop the ability to gauge the audience's reactions and adjust your presentation accordingly, you will be a much more effective speaker.

The following are tips on how to use your eyes effectively.

1. *Know your material.* Know it so well that you don't have to devote your mental energy to the task of remembering the sequence of ideas and words.

You should prepare well and rehearse enough so that you don't have to depend heavily on notes. Many speakers, no matter how well prepared, need at least a few notes to deliver their message. If you can speak effectively without notes, by all means do so. But if you must use notes, that's fine. Just don't let them be a substitute for preparation and rehearsal.

Even many experienced speakers use notes. Often, they take advantage of such natural pauses as audience laughter or the aftermath of an important point to glance briefly at their notes. To make this technique work, keep your notes brief.

2. *Establish a personal bond with listeners.* How do you do this? Begin by selecting one person and talking to him or her personally. Maintain eye contact with that person long enough to establish a visual bond (about 5 to 10 seconds). This is usually the equivalent of a sentence or a thought. Then shift your gaze to another person.

In a small group, this is relatively easy to do. But, if you're addressing hundreds or thousands of people, it's impossible. What you can do is pick out one or two individuals in each section of the room and establish personal bonds with them. Then each listener will get the impression you're talking directly to him or her.

3. *Monitor visual feedback.* While you are talking, your listeners are responding with their own non-verbal messages. Use your eyes to actively seek out this valuable feedback. If individuals aren't looking at you, they may not be listening either. Their reasons may include one or more of these factors:

a) They may not be able to hear you.

Solution: If you are not using a microphone, speak louder and note if that works.

b) They may be bored.

Solution: Use some humour, increase your vocal variety or add powerful gestures or body movements.

c) They may be puzzled.

Solution: Repeat and/or rephrase what you have just said.

d) They seem to be fidgeting nervously.

Solution: You may be using distracting mannerisms. Maybe you have food on your clothes (or worse, maybe your blouse is unbuttoned or your fly isn't closed). Make sure you are aware of these embarrassing possibilities before and during your speech. If necessary, try to correct them without bringing more attention to them. On the other hand, if your listeners' faces indicate pleasure, interest and close attention, don't change a thing. You're doing a great job!

Diction Tips

Because your speech content may be great, you may look fantastic but unless your audience can *understand* what you're saying, your message is lost.

Diction exercises will help you learn how to speak clearly. The athlete does warm-ups and stretches before an event: a singer does likewise. These exercises are the speaker's warm-up equivalent. They prepare and train you to speak with ease.

The specific benefits of diction/articulation exercises are:

a) strengthening and stretching the muscles involved in speech

b) bringing to your attention habitual speech patterns which may be less than perfect!

Good diction is not about changing your accent or making you 'talk posh'. It is about clarity - making sure what you say is heard.

The most commonly known and used Diction Exercises are Tongue Twisters.

There are thousands of them each focusing on either a single letter, or a letter combination. They are popular, fun and extremely effective.

Always start your diction exercises slowly and carefully. Make sure the beginning and end of each word is crisp and avoid running the words together.

A few examples of tongue twisters are given below. Repeat the phrase, getting faster and faster.

1. Six thick thistle sticks.
2. Betty bought a bit of butter, but she found the butter bitter, so Betty bought a bit of better butter to make the bitter butter better.
3. Did Doug dig Dick's garden or did Dick dig Doug's garden?
4. Four furious friends fought for the phone.
5. How was Harry hastened so hurriedly from the hunt?
6. James just jostled Jean gently.
7. My cutlery cuts keenly and cleanly.
8. Larry sent the latter a letter later.
9. Peter Piper picked a peck of pickled peppers. If Peter Piper picked a peck of pickled peppers, where's the peck of pickled peppers that Peter Piper picked?
10. Quickly, quickly, quickly, quickly, quickly...
11. Round the rugged rocks the ragged rascal ran.
12. Ten tame tadpoles tucked tightly in a thin tall tin.
13. Vincent vowed vengeance very vehemently.

And lastly, two especially for your tongue.

1. Red leather, yellow leather...
2. Red lorry, yellow lorry...

Develop an expressive speaking voice. Never be boring to listen to again.

How to Use Humour Effectively

(A good joke is very good. A bad one can be devastating.) Some folk choose not to learn how to use humour effectively for a very good reason. They are afraid. When a good laugh turns ugly it can explode in ways they never dreamed of. They feel attempting to learn how to use humour effectively is similar to tip-toeing through a live mine field barefoot. At any moment their carefully rehearsed joke or nifty one-liner could explode causing complete destruction of a presentation. Rather than risk it, they decide to err on the safe side and become a humour-free zone.

While their fear is understandable as nobody likes or actively seeks public melt-downs, it doesn't have to be that way.

You can learn how to use humour effectively.

Yes, it is risky. Yes, you might trip occasionally.

But one or two slips are hardly fatal and unless you risk you will never experience the joy of bringing humour to an audience.

Humour breaks through barriers- laughter can transcend age, race, gender, belief or class barriers. It relaxes your audience and puts them in a receptive mood. After you have made them laugh they are more likely to want to listen to you!

Humour alerts your audience to listen. They become more interested in what you're saying, than what happened prior to them listening to you or what is going to happen afterward. It brings your audience into the NOW!

Laughter adds 'juice' to a presentation. It can enliven potentially dry or dull material.

Humor releases tension. It binds people together. Almost every profession has its own humour. For instance, there are lawyer, teacher, doctor, and computer jokes. I'm sure with dedicated searching you could find jokes or humor about any type of employment.

The fears around using humour can be managed. When you've learnt how to use it effectively, you will have minimised the possibility of the laugh falling flat at your feet.

Given below are tips that help you to use humour effectively.

1. Know Your Audience

Never ever plan a joke without knowing who will be in your audience. To make humor work you need to know the approximate age of your audience and their general interests.

A joke told without knowledge of the audience because you think it is funny or humorous is dangerous. They are the ones most likely to explode.

How do you know they won't find it offensive? How do you know they'll understand it at all?

Humour varies from person to person and group to group. What we find funny is not a reliable indication that everyone else will find the same humour amusing.

If you don't know who your audience is FIND OUT!

Always integrate any joke you make into your speech or presentation. If you're telling the joke because you think it's a good one and bound to get you laughs BUT it has NOTHING to do with your speech topic, LEAVE IT OUT. It might be hilarious but it is not relevant. Unless you find a plausible, believable way to link the humour into your subject, forget it.

And if you do want to tell a joke or add humour and it is relevant make sure it is not introduced along the lines of:

'Have you heard the one about...?'

'This is really funny. You're going to howl with laughter.'

'There was this Irishman/Indian/Australian...'

None of these openings show the humour is blended with your own material and the second one is particularly nasty if your audience sits poker faced! The bottom line is: unless you were briefed to be a comedian, don't attempt it. This doesn't mean don't use humour. It means stick to your speech's purpose and find the humour from within that subject matter. The audience is not expecting a stand-up comedy routine.

2. *Always Use Safe Humour*

Use humour that doesn't use the audience as the butt of the joke. This is not the time to make jokes about. Use humour that doesn't isolate one segment of the audience as the butt of your remarks: blondes, males, females...anything that separates and sets one group up to laugh at another.

Use humour that doesn't rely on coarse language or profanity to make its point.

Use humour that avoids taboo subjects: religion, politics, race, class or sex.

How to use humor effectively often means using yourself as the subject but in a kindly way, making sure it is relevant to the subject.

Nobody wants to hear or see you putting yourself down consistently. You may laugh at your foibles or quirks publicly but not prostrate yourself for a whipping in front of an audience. That will embarrass them. When you laugh at yourself in a balanced, truthful way you are giving the audience permission to laugh with you, not at you. You are also inviting them to identify with you. This creates openness and trust. The audience will be more likely to listen because you're reflecting or showing them an aspect they know to be true of themselves as well as you.

Ask yourself have you earned the right to make the joke or use the humour about a particular situation.

Example:

An over weight person may make comments about being large.

A disabled person can joke about the difficulties they encounter on a daily basis.

A woman can laugh about the trials of child bearing provided she has had a child.

Always weave your jokes or humour into a small story or anecdote related to your topic. And keep the ratio of laugh to information balanced appropriately for the style of speech.

For example: if your speech is primarily to entertain rather than inform, it may be appropriate to use more humour. Judge the situation carefully.

Remember the 'rule of three'.

The rule of three works in all areas of presentation. It can be three examples to illustrate a point. It could three repetitions of the same word or phrase for emphasis, a device often used in oratory or three characters in an anecdotal story (an Irishman, Australian and American!). Three in storytelling is a naturally believable number whether you words to describe people and their actions or the events themselves. The first usage sets whatever it is up in the audience's mind as possibly believable. The second reinforces it and by the time the third instance comes along, the audience has accepted it as truth. Three, works! It is better to have several strong anecdotes in your presentation rather than a string of weak ones.

Always rehearse and test the humour you plan to use. To test have several people listen and give you honest feedback. Listen to the feedback. It maybe the subject is wrong for the situation, or perhaps your delivery needs work, or the tone of language choice needs altering.

All humour is based on two fundamental premise:

a. that COMEDY IS TRUTH

b. that COMEDY IS UNEXPECTED

Part of learning how to use humour effectively is to make it believable by introducing it as a part of the general flow of your speech. This makes it truthful in the ears and eyes of your audience. It also sets up the element of surprise as the audience will not be expecting the comedic twist.

Use an expressive voice. Live into the story you are telling to make it seem as if it were happening again. This gives the audience the 'feel' of the situation. They will grasp the situation and the emotional content more quickly.

Use simple pared down language. The less complicated the set-up and story, the more direct it is. The briefer and more explicit, the better, which is why a vast number of jokes start with stereotypical situations and characters. The teller does not have to explain them to the audience in order to be understood. Everybody knows what is being talked about immediately and they can get on with the story.

3. Practise Telling Your Story in as Many Ways as You can.

This is an essential step in learning how to use humour effectively.

What happens if you speed up here, and slow down there?

What happens if you emphasise this word instead of that word?

As a general rule comedians point up the punch line. They provide a cue to the audience that it is coming and prepare them to listen and laugh by a combination of slowing down, pausing and emphasis. It's called finding 'the beat'. Miss it and nobody will laugh. Find it and the same joke that previously bombed will fly. The only sure fire way to locate it is through practice. After enough, you'll sense it and know when to slow, pause and stress a word.

4. Use a Recorder to Listen to Yourself

This too, is an invaluable step in learning how to use humour effectively.

Is your lead-in smooth?

Is your voice expressive?

Is your language simple, effective and easily understood?

Have you pointed up the laugh line?

Is the laugh line clear?

Are you funny or is the story you are telling funny? For example, a comedian who has learnt how to use humor effectively, does not laugh at his own jokes as it breaks the illusion of truth. When you laugh at your own material you are on the outside of it, looking in, rather than BEING it.

5. Use Simple Large Gestures

If you are going to incorporate acting into your story practise using clear decisive gestures rather than a flurry of small ones. Involve your whole body in the action. Remember gestures need to be integrated with your speech to work.

Everybody, regardless of who they are or the language they speak, understands the body language of weeping in despair, pulling your hair out in desperation, or swooning with love. If you are prepared to work at it, gestures add a great deal in using humour effectively.

Types of Verbal Humour

Varying types of verbal humour are used liberally by comedy writers to spice their work. You can use them too.

1. ***Pun:*** a play on words, in which a word of multiple meanings or a word of similar sound but different meaning is used to create the joke.

Examples:

Heard about the fight down town? It was called a shopping maul.

Old teachers never die. They simply lose their class.

2. *Innuendo/Double Entendres:* an indirect, often derogatory hint. The speaker appears innocent and the innuendo is 'discovered' in mind of the listener. The most common of these are sexual innuendos.

Examples:

Mae West's 'Is that a gun in your pocket or are you just pleased to see me?'

The use of the word 'it' as in 'Comedians do it standing up.'

3. *Malapropism:* either intentional or unintentional misuse of a word created by using one of a similar sound for another.

Examples:

My sister has extra-century perception.

He was a man of great statue.

4. *Spoonerism:* an either intentional or unintentional transposition of sounds of two or more words.

Examples:

'nosey little cook' instead of 'cosy little nook'

'our queer old Dean' instead of 'our dear old Queen'

'I'm a damp stealer' instead of 'I'm a stamp dealer.'

5. *Mixed Metaphor:* to mix common sayings to comic effect.

Example:

'With friends like these, who needs enemas?'

6. *Joke:* Something said or done to evoke amusement or laughter. Mostly joke means an amusing story with a punch line.

Example:

A mother mouse and a baby mouse were walking along, when all of a sudden, a cat attacked them. The mother mouse goes, "BARK!" and the cat runs away. "See?" says the mother mouse to her baby. "Now do you see why it's important to learn a foreign language?"

7. ***Extended or Running Gag:*** an amusing situation or line recurring throughout a story or performance.

Example:

'The Goon Show', a famous British radio comedy show, had the line 'He's fallen in the water' running through all its episodes.

8. *Shaggy—dog Story:* a long rambling story filled with irrelevant detail and repeated phrases, which has an absurd anti-climatic punch line. It leads its listeners on in the expectation there will be an ending to make sense of all they've heard. Often there isn't or there will be a really weak pun. Its pointlessness is the joke!

9. *Parody:* to copy or imitate for comic affect the style of something or someone else. By its nature parody exaggerates and mocks the original. It only works if the person or thing being copied is well known to the audience.

Example:

The variations on The Ten Commandments.

I've seen 'Ten Commandments' for Cooks, Children, Wives, Husbands, Shopkeepers...

10. *Satire:* to expose silliness, foolishness or stupidity through ridicule. Satire attacks with the aim of alerting its audience and to make way for reform. The form has its roots in antiquity and is seen today in many forms. The television comedies 'The Simpsons' and 'South Park' use satire.

11. *Irony:* using language to imply the opposite of their literal meaning or a situation where the outcome is the opposite from that intended or expected.

    Irony and sarcasm are often regarded as being synonymous.

However sarcasm generally implies a stronger or more cutting remark and contains intent to ridicule unkindly.

Example of verbal irony:

'What pleasant weather!'—said while walking through a hailstorm.

Example of situational irony:

The plumber whose taps at home leak or the teacher's child who plays truant.

Example of sarcasm:

Mary is a thoroughly delightful woman with a delightful figure, a delightful dress sense, a delightful brain and an equally delightful husband to match. So much delight is entirely overwhelming and I must decline her invitation to dinner.

12. ***Understatement:*** deliberate minimising whatever is being spoken about. The audience knows and that is what makes the humour.

Example:

George is well known for his small appetite. Dinner consists of a mere half dozen pies, followed by large tub of ice-cream.

13. ***Overstatement:*** deliberate maximising of subject often with hyperbolic exaggeration.

Examples:

She is the most beautiful woman in the entire universe.

I am so hungry I could eat a horse.

14. ***Statement of the Obvious:*** a technique funny because it is so obvious or the expected norm.

Examples:

Cars have wheels.

People have two feet, two arms...

The sun is in the sky.

15. ***Exclusive Humour:*** using humour specific to a particular group of people for example in a workplace, players of a sport or members of a race. Outsiders find it hard to understand because they do not share the experience base from which it is drawn. It often has its own vocabulary (jargon) as well.

16. ***Absurdity:*** humour obviously lacking in reason. It is foolish or ridiculous and often includes the use of nonsensical language. In absurdity, the preposterous, incongruous, fantastical and whimsical are right at home.

Examples: the television shows, 'Monty Python's Flying Circus', and 'The Simpsons'

Some people use physical humour basics naturally. They can't help themselves. These are the folk who mimic either themselves or others as they tell their stories. Their arms will stretch as wide as possible to show you how big the fish was they caught. They will hop on one foot and grimace with exaggerated pain as they regale you with the story of how they stubbed their toe on the step while carrying the groceries inside.

People learn better with laughter. Good humor relaxes. It opens people...makes them more receptive and able to grasp new things or ideas. They will also remember longer if they learnt with laughter as the teacher.

The persons who can laugh at themselves publicly are admired.

Physical humour basics cuts through language and cross-cultural barriers faster than any speech can. The ability to mime is a great tool to have in your kit.

Physical humour appeals to all age groups. Each of us has a child within. We all remember the joy of seeing a clown at work.

Physical humour basics paints a picture and a picture says a thousand words.

The capacity to mime or reproduce stereotypical states of mind or people cuts out having to explain everything. Showing or demonstrating does it for you.

Mimicry can be cruel. Make sure you're creating safe/healthy laughter. That is you are not setting someone up to be laughed at. Use yourself as the butt of your humour if in doubt.

The 3 genres of physical humour below are often entwined.

1. *Slapstick:* a boisterous comedy with chases and collisions and practical jokes. Slapstick is an ancient form of humour involving as well as chases and collisions, highly exaggerated violence. Because the violence goes far beyond what is easily recognized as common sense, it becomes non-threatening and funny. Modern examples of comedians who use it are Rowan Atkinson, Mel Brooks and Jackie Gleason. Amongst professionals it is considered one of the more difficult forms to use as it relies on split second timing and finely honed characterisations to get the laughs.
2. *Farce:* a break-neck paced form of comedy relying on improbable situations, highly exaggerated characters and physical buffoonery. It incorporates much of slapstick with the addition of verbal wit usually in the form of puns and sexual innuendo. Farce is the basis of many popular sitcoms.
3. *Clowning/Mime:* both these forms have a long and distinguished history in the evolution of theatre. Clowning and mime skills depend on accurate as well as exaggerated characterisations of people. They are physically based rather than verbal and performers are often expected to be acrobatic as well. Traditionally a clown can juggle, do the splits, walk a tight rope, back flip and act. Their expertise is celebrated in circuses, theatre and on film and television. Many successful comedians use elements of clowning or mime in their

performances. Examples from the early silent days of film are the Charlie Chaplin and Laurel and Hardy movies.

Using Effective Pauses

When you use silence effectively you gain the Power of the Pause.

A pause in the right place at the right time gives YOU:

a. time to breathe

b. time to consider what it is you're going to say next

c. time to receive, digest and the feedback you're getting from your audience

A pause in the right place at the right time gives YOUR AUDIENCE:

a. time to breathe

b. time to let the images or ideas you've given them 'flower' in their minds

c. time to summarise what's been said

d. time to prepare for what may be coming next

There are differing types of pauses or silence.

What I'm not talking about are the Panic Pauses. These are the unplanned 'Oh, My Goodness!' variety. They come unexpectedly like thieves and whip our words away. They leave us gulping and grasping for a way to get back to the safety of what we thought we had prepared. And worse still, they seem to last for ever. Panic pauses need eradication. They have no place in your speech!

Planned Pauses are a different story. They are your friend. Used with care, the silences of your speech will be golden. And what's more they add rhythm or a beat to your words.

With practice, you will 'sense' the need to pause and how long to make it.

Like the speaking rate, diction, tone, pitch and volume exercises, these tips on using silence add another dimension, enriching your public speaking skills.

Have fun. Don't stress yourself trying to get it all right in one practice. Be gentle but firm. Remember habitual speech patterning is a challenge to change. It's regular effort that succeeds.

Let Punctuation Be Your Guide.

In printed text of any sort punctuation is used to separate words. The varying punctuation marks give information about how we should read and comprehend them. They arrange the words in parcels, separating one unit from the next, so we can easily unwrap/decode them one at a time. In short, punctuation allows us to make sequential sense of printed material.

In speech, punctuation marks are implied in the way we deliver our words.

Practice on a wider range of ordinary material. Read recipes or instruction sheets aloud making sure you give time for the audience to understand the sequence of actions needed to complete the tasks. Try informative articles on subjects you're interested in.

Remember silence is a gift you give to your self and your audience. Used effectively it can speak louder than your words. How? In stillness your words flower to their full potential. When speak you seed the thought or image. In the pause it grows.

Public Speaking Gaffes

Getting past the oops moment: Taking the podium

You're giving a career-making presentation to the whole company. The computer with your PowerPoint slides malfunctions.

Don't fiddle with your computer in front of an audience. If it's not fixed in two minutes, ask for a short recess.

Use humuor. The audience will be as uncomfortable about your contretemps as you, so loosen everyone up with a joke.

Walk around to make sure everyone can hear you. Getting physically closer to the audience will focus their attention on what you're saying.

Adapt. Poll the audience by hollering out questions.

"If something goes wrong, it's not a reflection of the person's ability. But someone who can adapt and recover—that's a skill, and it says a lot about their ability to think on their feet."

Colouring your voice: If you speak in a bland gray monotone you risk boring your listeners! They switch their ears off.

To give a successful oral presentation or speech you need an effective speaking voice. If you haven't got one you run the risk of boring your listeners. In essence, you're asking them to put up with second-rate service. The audience IS your customer. If they fidget, talk to their neighbours, gaze out the window, doodle on their note pads, leave...what does that tell you?

Your speech content could be excellent. It could match your audience's needs very well but unless you deliver it in an interesting way, you risk losing them.

A monotone voice is boring. It turns people off. An expressive energised voice keeps them turned on. Vocal variety is achieved through combining pitch, tone, volume and rate.

To understand pitch, think of music. It has high and low notes as do people's voices. Everyone's voice has a natural pitch. Women's tend to be higher than men's and everybody has a pitch range: the number of notes we habitually use. When that range is very small, the effect is monotonous.

Tone refers to the emotional content carried by our voices. It is not the words themselves, but 'how' we say them. To speak expressively, is to fill or energise our words appropriately.

For example, a person who puts very little energy into his speech, no matter what he is saying, is often described as being 'flat'. By contrast someone who fills his speech to overflowing with energy is described as being 'exuberant' or 'enthusiastic'.

How loudly or quietly you speak is called volume. Some people are habitually loud and others, quiet

The term 'rate' refers to speaking pace. How fast or slow do you speak? Can you vary the rate? Do you know the effect of slowing deliberately?

The goal for every speaker is: to find the most appropriate expression to meet the audience's needs.

And to match those needs with the content of the speech.

Take a deep breath in and begin speaking on whatever topic you choose until you run out of breath. It could be what is in front of you in the room, or out the window, what you had for breakfast...anything. Remain on the SAME note all the time. When you have finished, choose another note. It could be higher or lower and repeat. Pay careful attention to the effect it has on you! Notice the difference when you pitch your voice higher and then lower. You should feel a physical difference as well as an emotional one.

Say the sentences below in your high, middle and low pitch range. Note what happens to the intensity and the way you perceive the emotional content of the sentences. There will be a distinct variation between each.

Practice breathing using your diaphragm: Stand in front of a mirror. Make sure your feet are a comfortable shoulder-width apart. Pull yourself up straight and let your head sit square on your neck. Place one hand on your stomach. Breathe in. You should feel your stomach rising and then breathe out. This time your stomach falls. Watch your shoulders. If they rise and fall noticeably you are most likely breathing off the top of your lungs! Try until you can feel a definite rise and fall of your stomach. Keep relaxed.

If you feel any tension in your throat or chest from forcing the sound, stop. Breathe and begin again.

It helps to imagine the sound arcing through the air, in a concentrated focused stream to reach its target. The further away you get the more control you need to have over the outflow of air carrying your words.

Laugh out loud. Stand in front of your mirror breathing easily. On your out breath begin a series of Ha-ha-ha-ha's until all your breath is used. Take an in breath and start again. Vary your laughter. Make it louder, make it quiet and then build it up again. Repeat until you are laughing loudly and easily without any strain.

Read out loud. Make sure your stance and breathing is good. Pin point a place at the far end of your room to talk to.

Read aloud from your text, making sure you maintain your relaxed state while using as much vocal variety as you can.

A good way to test you're working as you should is to do this exercise with a partner. Have him stand at the far end of the room you're practising in. Give instructions to give you feedback on clarity, variety and pitch.

If you find yourself rising in pitch, check your breathing. When we tense, we strain the throat and when that happens our vocal chords are restricted. The result is we force the pitch up and limit the range or colour we can put into our words.

If you haven't got a partner available, be very aware of the changes in your body as you tighten. You will feel the strain in your upper chest and throat. In addition your shoulders will lift and you will run yourself out of breath easily.

Aim for control over one or two aspects at a time. Remember it's not so much the length of time you practice but the regularity. Ten minutes once a day over several weeks is more effective than an intense hour-long session once in a blue moon.

Check your speed pf speech delivery. If you've ever been called a motor-mouth, you'll know it's because the words rocket out of your mouth. That may be fun and exciting to listen to for a while but too much speed is dangerous. It can kill your speech. How? The people listening get tired. You may be asking them to work too hard. When your speech stops being stimulating and starts being uncomfortable, ears switch off.

And exactly the same thing happens at the other end of the spectrum. Slow word-by-very-slow-word turns ears off just as fast. Now people are waiting-and-waiting for you to get on with it and your lack of speed causes them to lose interest.

For the motor-mouths reading this consider:

Your listeners may interpret your haste as saying: 'I haven't got time for you.'

Or they may think you're telling them: 'I want this speech over and done with. It's a chore rather than a pleasure. I'll do it as fast as I can to be shot of it.'

Or they might think your unspoken message is: 'If you can't keep up with me and understand, it's you rather me with the problem. If you were more intelligent or focused you wouldn't have any difficulty.'

Or perhaps they're receiving: 'I'm feeling so anxious about speaking to you. I'm afraid you won't like or be interested in what I've got to say, or that I'll stuff it up so I'll say it as fast as possible and sit down.'

This is a common first-time or novice speaker reaction. It afflicts all sorts of people: students who have to give a presentation, new teachers, actors...The cure is to acknowledge your fear, deal with it appropriately and keep on speaking.

For the habitually slow speakers consider:

Your careful word-by-word placement may insult your listeners. It may make them feel you think they're so dull or silly they will not be able to grasp your content if you go any faster.

Your listeners may think you are boring. Slow is often equated with lack of passion so they might decide you are not particularly interested in either them or your topic.

The audience might feel you don't really know what you are talking about. You have to go slowly because you are searching for each new word or idea.

The answer to the fast-slow problem is not the middle ground. Rather it is to vary our speaking rate in direct response to our audience's and our content's need.

Picture in your mind the layout of your speech. You'll have an introduction, followed by a series of main ideas with supporting examples or illustrations. To finish there'll be a conclusion. Now think of the thread (theme, main idea) linking it altogether. It is similar to a road. You are taking your audience on a journey. Your speech is the vehicle carrying them along and your mouth is the driver.

As the driver you make choices. You can whirl them through so fast the scenery blurs. While you're busy negotiating a series of complicated hairpin bends at full throttle, they're gazing out of the back window trying to work out what they've missed and where they are. One by one your listeners get dizzy. Then they close off their ears and sit quietly waiting for the ride to stop.

Or by contrast you can proceed so cautiously your passengers want to get out and walk.

If you were a responsive driver you would be continually adjusting your speed to meet the road conditions and the needs of your passengers. There would be places to slow and perhaps even stop for the audience to catch their breath. There would also be places where a quick burst of acceleration would give an exciting thrill.

Generally a faster-speaking speed signals urgency, excitement, passion or raw emotion. It can lead the audience to expect something thrilling is going to occur. They hold their breaths and go for the ride with you.

In contrast a slower-speaking rate signals importance, seriousness, or significant ideas. A new concept or new and perhaps, complex sequential information may need to be delivered slowly so the audience has time to grasp all of the ideas and their consequences before moving on. 'Slow' is also useful for summarising material.

The combination of slow, fast, slow, medium speed, etc., adds interest to your speech making it easier to listen to.

Read or recite part of a text you know and love quickly. If you can record yourself, do so. If not, listen and note the effect it has on you. If you've recorded yourself, play it back. Ask yourself where was the speed effective? Where was it detrimental? Mark those places on your script.

Time yourself reading or saying your speech at your normal speaking rate. Note the time down. Now go through again having marked passages for slower or faster treatment. Note the new time.

Listen to speakers you admire. They could be radio presenters, preachers...anybody accustomed to speaking in public. Note the different rates of speech they use over the course of their presentation and the effectiveness of them. (Try to listen to a variety so you have a broad range to draw inspiration from.) Take elements of their rate changes and experiment with them for yourself.

And lastly, give yourself a pat on the back. Changing speaking rate is challenging. The habitual speed of words leaving our mouths is deeply ingrained. As children we are very effective sponges. We soak up everything around us, including the speech rates used by our significant adults. What was their normal speech speed becomes ours. It feels natural, comfortable and right! Altering rate is not impossible but it does require awareness, effort and practice!

Remember the picture of your mouth as the driver? When your tongue is high revving it's accelerating away. When you're stuck in first gear, it's crawling forward one little word at a time. Now you've got control over rate, it's time to turn your attention to the brakes. Skilled use of the brakes are the key to effective silence. Get Power in your Pause here!

Constructive Criticism

You can expect that your audience will be listening to your ideas and discerning whether your evidence supports your argument. As you advance a claim, your audience may well wonder how well you have made your case. Constructive criticism gives you feedback about how well you made your case, without destroying your confidence!

Communication experts George Grice and Bruce Skinner recommend the following excellent guidelines for critiquing speeches:

1. Begin with a positive statement.
2. Target a few key areas for improvement.
3. Organise your comments.
4. Be specific.
5. Be honest but tactful.
6. Personalise your comments.
7. Reinforce the positive.
8. Problem-solve the negative.
9. Provide the speaker with a plan of action.
10. End with a positive statement.

As you give feedback to others, consider carefully whether your feedback is warranted, balanced, timely, and solicited. Learn from expert speakers. Talk with expert speakers and learn from them! Watch great speakers and discover their secrets for planning, practicing and presenting excellent talks.

Watch and consult with professional speakers to learn how they plan, practise and present a talk. Work with public speaking support groups.

Volunteer to speak. There are countless opportunities for you to give talks in business, social, and personal contexts.

Whether it's a retirement, a sports banquet, wedding, or toast at a special dinner, you can use your speaking skills to make the occasion more special.

Consider the many times that you might agree to say a few words:

1. Your parents have an anniversary and you host a dinner party;
2. Your child is celebrating a special occasion (e.g. wedding, graduation);
3. Your boss is retiring;
4. Your sports team wins the cup and you earn the best sportsperson award;
5. You've been named citizen of the year in your community;
6. There is a piece of legislation that you strongly oppose;
7. Your boss wants you to explain your company policy to the press;
8. Your best friend needs a good speaker at the next club meeting;
9. You need to introduce a speaker to an audience.

While audience analysis and knowledge of the expectations of the speaking occasion is important for any form of public speaking, this is particularly true for special occasion talks.

Here are some important considerations:

1. Be positive.
2. Be brief.
3. Be gracious.
4. Be sincere.

7 Overcoming Stage Fright

The fear of public speaking is called glossophobia (or, informally, "stage fright"). It is believed to be the single most common phobia—affecting as much as 75 per cent of the population. Fear of oration is ranked even above that of death. As Jerry Seinfeld observes, the average person would rather be in the casket than doing the eulogy.

Don't be scared and just talk. Don't apologise for making a mistakes or being nervous.

Glossophobia may be linked to, or sometimes precede, a more severe anxiety disorder. Several talented and successful musicians have the fear of performing in public, including Peter Gabriel, Barbra Streisand, Kirsty MacColl and Dusty Springfield.

Symptoms include: intense anxiety prior to, or simply at the thought of having to verbally communicate with any group; avoidance of events which focus the group's attention on individuals in attendance; and physical distress, nausea, or feelings of panic in such circumstances.

Many people report stress-induced speech disorders that are only present during public speech. If you don't get up in front of an audience you never have to worry about stage fright. Some glossophobics have been able to dance or perform in public as long as they do not have to speak, or even speak (such as in a play) or sing as long as they cannot see the audience or they feel that they are a character or stage persona rather than presenting as themselves.

Impromptu or Extemporaneous Speaking

While many of us do not like to speak in front of people, there are times when we are asked to get up and say a few words about someone or a topic when we have not planned on saying anything at all. We are more shocked than anyone else. Has this ever happened to you? If and when this does happen to you, be prepared to rise to the challenge. Below are some tips you can use the next time you are called on to speak.

Decide quickly what your one message will be. Keep in mind you have not been asked to give a speech but to make some impromptu remarks. Hopefully they have asked you early enough, so you can at least jot down a few notes before you speak. If not, pick one message or comment and focus on that one main idea. Many times, other ideas may come to you after you start speaking. If this happens, go with the flow and trust your instincts.

Do not try and memorise what you will say. Trying to memorise will only make you more nervous, and you will find yourself thinking more about the words and not about the message.

Start off strong and with confidence. If you at least plan your opening statement, this will get you started on the right foot. After all, just like with any formal speech, getting started is the most difficult. Plan what your first sentence will be. You may even write down this opening line on your note card and glance at it one more time just before you begin speaking. If you know you have three points or ideas to say, just start off simply by saying, "I would just like to talk about 3 points". The first point is... the second point is... and so on.

Decide on your transitions from one point to the other. After you have decided on your opening remark or line, come up with a simple transition statement that takes you to your main point. If you have more than one point to make, you can use a natural transition such as, "My second point is... or my next point is..." etc. Just list it down on your note card or napkin, if you have to, the main points or ideas. Do not write out the exact words, but just the points you want to mention.

Maintain eye contact with the audience. This is easier to do if you do not write down all kinds of stuff to read. Look down at your next idea or thought and maintain eye contact with your audience; speak from your heart. Focus on communicating to your audience and not speaking at the crowd.

Occasionally throw in an off-the-cuff remark. Because you want your style to be flexible and seem impromptu, trust your instinct and add a few words that just pop into your head. Keep it conversational and think of the audience as a group of your friends.

Finally, have a good conclusion. Gracefully just state, "And the last point I would like to make is ...". Once you have made your last point, you can then turn control back to the person who asked you to speak in the first place.

With a little practice, this process will feel more natural to you. Anticipating that you may be asked to say a few words should force you to at least think about what you might say if you are asked. Then if you ARE asked, you are better prepared because you anticipated being asked. This is much better than thinking they won't ask you and they actually do!

Overcoming Performance Anxiety

These tips for overcoming performance anxiety or fear of public speaking remove the need to battle the fight or flight syndrome head on.

Do you want more information about the fight or flight response? Or maybe you're unsure whether you are suffering from performance anxiety due to fear of public speaking?

With just a little time invested in following a few carefully chosen suggestions, you'll be on your way to being a much less stressed speaker. And that feels a whole lot better than being the victim of an ancient set of rampant instinctive responses! Get the adrenalin flowing in your body working for you by sidestepping into systematic planning. This way, when and if it does peak, it will have a well-rehearsed pathway to run down. You will have those nerves under control and contained.

1. Get all the facts.
2. Know where the performance/speech is scheduled to happen.
3. Know precisely when you are required to be there.
4. Find out how long you are expected to speak.
5. If you don't know or haven't been told, find out what subject matter is suitable.
6. Get an estimate of the expected size of the audience and who they are likely to be (male, female, mixed audience, old, young, mixed age range and any other pertinent defining characteristics).
7. Make sure you *write it all down* and put somewhere you know you'll not lose it: place, date, time, length of speech, subject, audience and the name of your contact person from the organisation or group you're speaking for, plus their phone number.

Breathing Exercises

Breathing exercises will effectively, simply and quickly ease your tension. They release fear, lower stress levels and enhance your speaking voice.

Anxiety makes us 'uptight' in more ways than one. If you're familiar with the expression you'll know it generally applies to 'being snappy' or 'short tempered'. But being uptight is not only the temporary absence of our usually relaxed easy-going selves.

It is also what literally happens physically.

Under stress we tighten our muscles and hole the tension we're feeling. It locks itself into our bodies. The cumulative effect of long-term unreleased tension is varying forms of debilitating and often fatal illnesses.

One of the first places tension shows is in our breathing patterns. Anxiety makes us breathe more quickly and less deeply. The result is the body perceives itself as being under threat and the automatic primitive survival mechanism fight or flight response takes over.

The physiological effects of anxiety include: breathing off the tops of our lungs which in turn gives rise to less oxygen circulating in our system, a build up of carbon monoxide (because it's not being released through full exhaling), and in some people, panic attacks or hyperventilation

The direct consequence of anxiety on the quality of your voice is losing control of pitch and tone.

Shallow breathing means you restrict the fullness of sound and range your voice might have. It will sound squeezed or strained because you are talking off the top of your lungs with a tight throat, jaw, mouth and face.

Forcing your voice to override the restrictions is not an answer. It causes damage ranging from reasonably mild inconveniences like a sore throat to serious problems requiring surgical intervention.

Consistently being fearful and therefore breathing shallowly can become a vicious cycle. The less air we take in, the worse we feel and the less effectively we speak. The less effectively we speak, the worse we feel, and the less air we take in.

The only way to break the cycle is to learn and use good breathing habits. Try the following breathing exercises.

1. Stand with your feet a comfortable shoulder width apart.

Support the weight of your body through your hips and legs rather than locking your knees. Consciously release and relax your shoulders.

If you're holding your stomach in, let it go.

Place your hands on your stomach. Breathe in through your nose to the count of four. Count slowly. As you inhale feel your diaphragm rising.

Breathe out through your mouth to the count of four and now feel your diaphragm expanding.

Do several rounds of inhale and exhale to a four count while making sure you keep your shoulders, stomach and legs relaxed.

Once you have mastered the four count, increase it.

Through regular practice you will soon be able to extend it for a eight or even ten count. By then you will be feeling relaxed, alert and ready.

2. Stand with your feet a comfortable shoulder width apart.

Support the weight of your body through your hips and legs rather than locking your knees.

Consciously release and relax your shoulders.

If you're holding your stomach in, let it go.

Bring your palms together in the centre of your chest.

As you slowly inhale through your nose, keeping the palms of your hands together, raise your arms as high as you can above your head. At the same time raise yourself on to your toes.

Hold your breath briefly at the top of your inhale, keeping yourself fully stretched and pushing without strain toward to the sky.

Exhale slowly through your mouth while keeping your arms fully extended. Bring them down and round back up to your chest, palms together in the starting position. At the same time slowly lower your feet.

Repeat for 10 Rounds

The benefits of both these exercises are immediate, psychologically and physically. Physiologically you are using all of your lungs rather than the top third and have more oxygen in your system. An additional benefit is you are strengthening your physical capacity to speak for a longer time, to deal with more complex patterns of language effectively and you won't need to break for breath as frequently. Make these breathing exercises a part of your daily voice warm-up routine. They're good for you.

In the midst of a crisis irrational fears may take over. Often they are quite without foundation. These belong in a murky underworld and cannot survive in the clear light of factual truth. Take a moment to ask yourself some searching questions and listen to the real answers.

Are you mistaking the ordinary adrenalin rush of excitement for fear?

Have you prepared carefully?

Have you 'survived' this type of feeling before?

If the answer to all questions is YES, do a deep breathing round and let the feelings go! If the answers are unclear or NO, do a deep breathing round! You haven't got time or energy to entertain this negativity. You've got things to organise, starting right now by getting your mind clear.

Resist Using Alcohol

Alcohol is a short term and unsatisfactory acute anxiety help solution. It may quell your nerves but it is far from being an acute anxiety help as it will also dull your ability to respond quickly and appropriately. It can lead to dependency if used long term.

Use Your Imagination Positively

Build huge multi-coloured vibrant pictures of yourself doing well. See yourself at ease. See yourself performing beautifully.

Make the images as detailed as possible. Add sound, smell, feel...Use all your senses to create an outstanding movie featuring yourself. See yourself before the performance, poised and alert. See yourself during it, responding to the challenge and see yourself afterward, reflecting on a task done well. Show yourself the pictures whenever you feel anxiety beginning to tighten its grip. Be sure to make them large and crystal clear! You could build a slide show into the breathing exercise for extra efficiency.

Sometimes we get so knotted having someone who cares for and understands us alongside is a great help. Tell them their chief task is to keep you on track. They may understand your anxiety but they are not to heighten it by playing into it. They are there to remind you to breathe, to see yourself as successful and be of practical assistance etc. Their first job is to banish anybody adding to your stress unnecessarily.

Eat Lightly

Heavy food in a delicate stomach makes you feel even more unwell. Eat light foods or if you can't eat anything, take a nourishing drink, like a banana shake. (In fact bananas have been found to contain natural beta blockers which minimise symptoms of anxiety.)

Be in the Moment

When you are 'in the moment' your mind is not racing ahead filling itself with all sorts of concerns about what might or could happen. Instead you are focused on what it is you are doing now and carrying out that activity to the very best of your ability. This makes you alert and responsive. To help you stay in the 'now' practise breathing fully. Use the rhythm of good breath control to anchor you.

Success Recall

One of the best antidotes to is to remember previous occasions when you felt and were successful. The more vividly you can recall them the more effective it will be. Remember what it felt like! It doesn't have to be the same as the situation you are preparing to meet now. The most important aspect of this exercise is experiencing yourself as a success!

Get a Massage

If you have the time make an appointment with a qualified massage practitioner. There are varying types of massage available all of which work to release tension stored in the body. Discuss what you need when you make the appointment. The practitioner will advise what will be beneficial.

Re-check Your Planning

Go through the 'little' details as these can be the things which in the end cause the most stress, simply because they are overlooked.

How are you getting to the venue?

What do you have to take?

Prepare everything well ahead of time so you arrive with nothing to do but perform.

Play Soothing Music

Baroque music is known for its calming effect. Its patterning actually alters the brain waves making them clearer and more ordered. Get some Bach or Vivaldi on your music machine now!

How to Create a Great First Impression

They say you can't judge a book by its cover but how many of us judge people by the way they talk, or even by the way they answer the telephone?

We form opinions about people the first time we see or hear them. We even form opinions about people we have never met!

People's "perception" about us does matter. We are all judged by people through "What we say", and "How we say it". We are also judged by "How we Dress", "How we walk" and even "How we eat our food".

In the work environment, we judge people by the size of their office, the location of their office or by the number of people working for us.

As a business owner your company is judged by the way your receptionist answers the telephone or greets people at the door.

Think about it!

You cannot fail to make a first impression. People always form an initial impression about us the first time they come in contact with us, whether it is in person or whether it is over the telephone or even by the way we leave a message on their answering machine. Every other contact with us after that first time either supports or conflicts with that first impression.

Create a good first impression and the relationship grows from there. Create a bad first impression and your relationship with that person can be an uphill battle.

Whether we are communicating "one-to-one" over the telephone, "one-to-a-group" such as a small business meeting or "one-to-a-hundred" such as during a presentation, other people's impressions of us is very important and we should work hard to make sure that first impression is a great one.

8 Personal Grooming and Body Language

Personal Grooming

Taking care of personal grooming for looking good is part of an effective speech.

Some say personal grooming is just that: personal. They go on to insist that personal matters are nobody else's concern than their own. Their personal grooming is their personal grooming. Other people can either like it or lump it as they see fit.

And therein lurks a potential problem. Everybody's personal grooming is not equal. There are generally agreed upon guidelines but their interpretation varies. Put a widely diverse bunch of people in a room and give them a quiz about personal grooming and they'll more than likely to agree on the basics: clean hair, shoes, tidy dress, etc. But get the same bunch of people to dress as if they were all going to give a similar speech at a similar venue to a similar audience and guess what? You already know the answer.

Personal grooming does have to be spelt out. And for those of you think it's a petty concern and only of interest to those who want to blend their individuality to bland, think again.

We know from research a person has approximately a few seconds to make an initial positive impact on strangers. While we may like to think we are not so 'shallow' or so easily influenced one way or another, we are. We judge people on their appearances. We do it all the time but we especially do it when we meet someone new. Bad hair day? Missed a bit of shaving? Sloppy shoeshine? We've noticed and logged it. We might not be totally conscious of ticking off the boxes on a personal grooming check list but the reality is, we have a sharpened pencil poised for action the moment we set eyes on them.

So what is on A Personal Grooming Checklist? - Face, Hair, Clothes, Shoes, Accessories, and so on. All of these elements combine to make the first important initial impression. To make it positive each has to work harmoniously with the other. But more than that, the total effect must be appropriate for the occasion.

Your goal is to present yourself attractively while not detracting from your purpose. Your task is to present a speech. Your choice of clothing and grooming should support that. Too much and your appearance gets all the attention. The same happens with too little effort. The result is the reception of your speech flounders.

Guidelines for Clothing, Shoes and Accessories

Clothing must be comfortable. You have to be able to breathe and move, so nothing too tight.

Clothes must be tidy. Check loose buttons, dodgy zips, hanging threads, hems that have come undone. And clothes must be freshly pressed or dry-cleaned.

Furthermore, those clothes must look all-of-a-piece: the skirt goes with the blouse, the shirt belongs with the trousers, the blouse matches the sari, the salwar-kameez and dupatta match.

Keep accessories simple. This is not the time to wear the string of little jingly brass bells brought back from a recent trip.

Shoes must be comfortable and freshly cleaned (avoid breaking in a new pair of shoes while standing to talk. It's painful!). If you wear slippers or sandals, ensure that they are comfortable and clean, not worn out and shabby.

Personal Grooming Preparation

Prepare everything you need several working days in advance. Go through your wardrobe to sort out the possibilities and try each of them on. Be sure to try the whole outfit, shoes and accessories included. Check each selected item for damage and cleanliness. If anything needs to go to the cleaners or be washed, do it.

If anything needs minor mending, do it. And do it sooner rather than later. You don't need the added hassle of trying to sew a button on while driving to the venue.

NOW turn your attention to your hair. Do you need a haircut or a trim and tidy up? Get that done earlier rather than later too.

Don't plan a radical change too close to your speech date. If you don't like the result, you might not have the time to do anything about it.

Choose a style you feel comfortable with, one that you do not have to worry about and lets you get on with your task.

A key consideration is making sure the audience can see all of your face. If you wear a long fringe, it may mask your eyes. Likewise long loose hair may cover your face while speaking.

The audience needs to 'read' your face while they listen to you talk. Covering or partially covering up makes the communication process harder. It may also send unintentional signals. The audience may interpret you as 'hiding behind your hair'. They may think you are avoiding them or very self-conscious and unsure of yourself. Some of that may be true but you don't need to advertise it. You're going to stand tall, face them: 'feel the fear and do it anyway'!

Wear a make-up that is appropriate to go with your clothes and the occasion. If you are going to be lit while talking you may need more than you usually wear. Stage lights can drain all the colour from your face. Get advice if you are unsure.

The final step in your personal grooming preparation is to have at least one full dress rehearsal wearing everything as you planned it. This will let you know whether or not your choices are suitable and comfortable. If you have to stop to push straps back where they belong or keep tucking in a shirt whose tail is too short, change your choice. These clothes will be distraction rather than an aid.

You're ready to go. Quite rightly your aim to be there with plenty of time to spare. You've done all the preparation. Your personal grooming is superb. You will pass the three-second positive impression test easily. Your speech is entertaining and informative. The audience is excitedly looking forward to your presentation.

Rid yourself of distracting mannerisms, like, finger tapping, lip biting or licking, adjusting hair or clothing, head wagging, toying with coins or pen/pencil, etc.

They are physical manifestations of simple nervousness, perhaps performed unconsciously.

When you make a verbal mistake, you can easily correct it, since you can hear your own words, but as you can't see yourself, your distracting mannerisms go uncorrected. You can't eliminate them unless you know they exist.

The first step in eliminating any superfluous behaviour is to obtain an accurate perception of your body's image. This should include: Posture, Gestures, Body movement, Facial expressions and Eye contact.

Go over the list of all the distracting mannerisms you see and hear while hearing a speech. The next time you are having a conversation with someone you know well, try to notice whether you use any of these distracting mannerisms even in casual circumstances. Tackle each of your negative points one at a time.

Your Appearance

If your listeners will have on suits and dresses, wear your best suit or dress—the outfit that brings you the most compliments. Make sure that every item of clothing is clean and well tailored.

Don't wear jewellery that might glitter or jingle when you move or gesture. This might divert attention from your speech. For the same reason, empty your pockets of bulky items and anything that makes noise when you move.

Part of the first impression you give occurs even before you are introduced to deliver your speech. As the audience arrives, your preparation should be concluded. You shouldn't have to study your speech. Instead, mingle with the audience, and project that same friendly, confident attitude that will make your speech a success.

When you speak, especially if you aren't well known to the audience, the most crucial part of your presentation is the first few minutes. During that initial segment, the audience will be making critical judgements about you. Your listeners will decide whether you are confident, sincere, friendly, eager to address them and worthy of their attention. In large measure, they will base this decision on what they see.

After your introduction, walk purposefully and confidently to the speaking position.

Walking Patterns

Why move in the first place? Moving forces people to focus and follow you. The way you walk from your seat to the speaker's position is very important. When you are introduced, you should appear eager to speak. Too many speakers look as though they are heading toward execution.

Walk confidently from your seat to the lectern. Pause there for a few seconds, then move out from behind the lectern. As discussed before, it is wise to use the lectern as a point of departure, and not a barrier to hide behind.

Smile before you say your first words. Be careful not to stand too close to, nor move beyond, the people in the front row. Be careful not to walk too much. Doing so will work against you. Continuous pacing is distracting. Walking can be an effective way to stress an important idea. It is essential that your walk be purposeful and intentional, not just a random shift of position. Taking about three steps, moving at a shallow angle, usually works best.

When employing visual aids, use three positions. One position is your "home" position and should be front and centre. The other two positions should be relatively near the "home" position. Never stand in front of any visual aid.

When you practise your speaking, make sure you also practise your walking patterns. Try walking to and from your three positions. These positions should be planned just as your hand gestures are.

When standing still, remember to maintain good posture. Stand up straight.

Remember it's not what you say, it's how you say it, and your body does speak very loudly. Only when you unite your verbal message and your non-verbal message do you begin to command presence as a speaker.

How to Gesture Effectively

Gestures are reflections of every speaker's individual personality. What's right for one speaker may not be right for another;

however, the following six rules apply to anyone who seeks to become a dynamic effective speaker.

1. Respond naturally to what you think, feel, and see. It's natural for you to gesture, and it's unnatural for you not to. If you inhibit your impulse to gesture, you will probably become tense.
2. Create the condition for gesturing, not the gesture. When you speak, you should be totally involved in communicating, not thinking about your hands. Your gestures should be motivated by the content of your presentation.
3. Suit the action to the word and the occasion. Your visual and verbal messages must function as partners in communicating the same thought or feeling. Every gesture you make should be purposeful and reflective of your words so the audience will note only the effect, not the gesture itself. Don't overdo the gesturing. You'll draw the listener away from your message. Young audiences are usually attracted to a speaker who uses vigorous gestures, but older, more conservative groups may feel irritated or threatened by a speaker whose physical actions are overwhelming.
4. Make your gestures convincing. Your gestures should be lively and distinct if they are to convey the intended impressions. Effective gestures are vigorous enough to be convincing yet slow enough and broad enough to be clearly visible without being overpowering.
5. Make your gestures smooth and well timed. Every gesture has three parts:
   a) The Approach—Your body begins to move in anticipation.
   b) The Stroke—The gesture itself.
   c) The Return—This brings your body back to a balanced posture.

The flow of a gesture—the approach, the stroke, the return—must be smoothly executed so that only the stroke is evident to the audience. While it is advisable to practise gesturing, don't try to memorise your every move. This makes your gesturing stilted and ineffective. The last rule is perhaps the most important but also the hardest.

6. Make natural, spontaneous gesturing a habit. The first step in becoming adept at gesturing is to determine what, if anything, you are doing now. The best way to discover this, is to videotape your self. The camcorder is completely truthful and unforgiving. If you want to become a better speaker, you need to make the camcorder your best friend.

Videotape yourself and identify your bad habits, then work at eliminating them, one at a time. You will need to continue to record yourself and evaluate your progress if you expect to eliminate all your distracting mannerisms.

To improve gestures, practise, but never during a speech. Practise gesturing while speaking informally to friends, family member, and coworkers.

Do you know the effect of your habitual gestures on your audience? You may be unconsciously undermining or lessening the impact of your speech with unnecessary distracting movement.

When you teach yourself body language you gain more control over how your presentation is received.

Do I really need to learn this? Maybe or maybe not.

Try a quick test to help you decide whether or not you need body language awareness.

Think of someone you know very well who is unaccustomed to public speaking.

Imagine they are in front of you now. What gestures or body stances do they habitually use? Do they rattle coins in their pockets? Or do they stroke their chin while thinking? Perhaps they shift from one foot to the other or fold their arms across their chests?

Now imagine that person standing in front of an audience giving a speech. If you didn't know them how would you interpret their body language?

Would you think they were nervous? Would you be put-off by all their fiddling?

Would you question their ability? Would you think if they're going to continue to talk in public they need a teach yourself body language course to help make them more aware of themselves?

And now, think of yourself. What do you do?

What would you see yourself doing if the camera was on you?

The brutal truth is we make a snap-judgement.

We give people approximately ten seconds or less to prove themselves interesting to us. Any habitual gestures that don't enhance communication serve as a block. They turn people off.

Successful speakers ooze confidence. They have successfully conquered any distracting habitual gestures they may have had. When they speak in public their body language effectively supports and reinforces their speech.

Given below are a few pointers for making them work easily and effectively for you.

1. Work in front of a full length dress mirror.
2. If you can video yourself do so. Playing it back will give your important feedback.
3. Go for mastery over one habit you want to modify or get rid of at a time rather than trying to banish the lot at once.
4. Remember, regular smaller practices are more effective than one or two intense longer workouts.

5. Practise what you can throughout the day. You do not need to wait until you are at home to practise standing well, or relaxing your shoulders.
6. Practise standing on two feet! It might seem basic but often people stand on one foot with the other tucked in behind the upright leg and then they swap over and the other foot has a turn. Soon it's the first foot's turn again and so on.
7. Practise standing 'at ease'. Place your feet about a comfortable shoulder width apart. Make sure you are standing on the whole of your foot so your feet are fully connected to the floor. This position supports all of your body while distributing your weight evenly through your hips and legs without undue stress. The body language of someone standing comfortably like this says: confidence, capable, control and balanced.
8. Practise standing tall. Pull yourself up to full height. Imagine a string running through you from the crown of your head to your feet. Now imagine that string being gently pulled toward the sky. Your back will straighten. Your neck will hold your head high. Notice the feel and look of standing straight. When you see other people standing similarly, you recognise them as being someone who feel good about themselves. They appear to have energy, presence and power.
9. Let your shoulders relax. Practise by rolling them backwards and forwards. Pretend they are a coat hanger from which your chest and arms hang. In order for them to hang well your shoulders need to be straight and relaxed.

   Raised shoulders can signal heightened tension, defensiveness as if you are waiting to fend off negativity or anxiety. Shoulders habitually slumped forward say 'depressed', 'defeated' or 'closed'.
10. Practise breathing deeply and evenly using your diaphragm while maintaining a fully upright relaxed stance. Notice how

open your chest is. Notice how your hips carry the weight of your upper body. Notice how your shoulders carry your arms but most of all notice how connected, strong and balanced you are.

11. The key to gesture is to keep it clear and appropriate. Many of us use a flurry of gestures. We wave our arms, point, clasp and unclasp our hands, fiddle with whatever we are holding, scratch our chins...The variations are infinite. Often what we are doing bears no real relationship to the subject matter of our speech. They become a distraction.
12. Practise speaking either clasping your hands loosely in front of you or with your arms at your side. Some people clasp their hands behind their back. Experiment with this too. However there is a tendency to lean forward which means you are not standing upright.
13. Practise gesture specifically related to your content. That is, if you are describing something huge, you could indicate size with your arms open wide. Or maybe you want to point to something on a chart. Use one clear, large gesture. (Large gestures are ones involving the whole body. For example: the arm moves out from the chest and is fully extended. Small gestures are those held more closely to the body. Because they are small they can be missed by your audience or misinterpreted.)
14. If you are confident you could even incorporate a little 'acting' into your presentation. This could be to take on a voice, a gesture to show your audience but only if it is appropriate to your content. Again it needs to be bold and clear so the audience can read it how you intended. Once the acting is done, you move straight back into your ordinary presentation style.
15. The eyes always have it! Think of all the expressions we habitually use referring to eyes, and you'll realise how

important they are in communication. We 'eye' someone up. We ask if someone 'sees' straight. We like getting a good 'eye-full'. The 'eyes are the windows to the soul' and seeing them is believing!

We want the person talking to us to look at us. We don't like it if they turn their heads away, if their eyes flicker from one side of us to the other, or look down. We want to be looked straight in the eye. It is only then that we feel met and communicated with clearly.

Interpretations of lack of eye contact are: shyness, lack of self esteem, shame, deceit, lying, extreme anxiety,etc.

16. Practise looking at your audience. Choose a person and meet their eyes briefly but long enough to know you have made contact. Choose another and do the same.

    Talking directly to one person as in maintaining the eye contact for too long is considered rude but shifting your focus through the members of your audience is good. It makes them feel met.

17. Another useful tip is to select a spot just above the heads of the audience at the far end of the place you are talking in. When you talk to it, it will appear as if you are talking to everybody, including those way at the back.

18. Practise looking from your notes to your audience. If you are reading, the temptation is to do just that. You stay head down for the whole of your talk. This is boring for your audience. And it is rude. You have people there who made an effort to be present. Ignoring them because you are reading will make them feel cut out or alienated.

19. Double space and number your notes. Use a clear font and mark the major points with a highlighter. This will lessen the possibility of losing your place when you look up to meet your audience.

20. One of the song goes as: 'When you're smiling, the whole world smiles with you.' It's true. A smile says 'I like being here. I like you.' As a speaker your smile communicates ease and confidence. It breaks the ice and lightens the mood. Practice smiling at the people you're talking to. You don't have to do it endlessly until your face hurts! (And if you do, your audience will assume there's something amiss with you!) But if you can manage one, two, three or more in appropriate places particularly coupled with eye contact, you'll be seen as a warm, approachable person.

21. Many of us pull faces. We may not be poking out our tongues or rolling our eyes but we're grimacing, biting our bottom lip and scrunching up our foreheads completely unaware of the effect it has on the people looking at us. We read faces constantly. We are looking for non-verbal cues to tell us who this person is. We want the sub-text. We want to know what is going on below the words but more than that we want to know if the words we are hearing match what we're seeing on the 'face'.

    What story is your face telling? Raised eyebrows may be saying: 'I don't believe that.' 'I doubt or I question what ever you are saying.' A scrunched forehead may say: 'I'm thinking hard' or 'I'm angry and stressed.' A wrinkled up nose signals distaste. 'I don't like whatever you've just told me or I've just seen.' Biting at your lips can be seen as anxiety or intense concentration. Tight lips can be seen as unwilling to share information or deliberate withholding. A rigid jaw is often interpreted as trying to keep things under control, particularly anger.

22. Practise consciously relaxing your face. Let the tightness in your forehead, cheeks, jaw, lips, and throat go. You'll be amazed how much better your face feels.

    To get rid of tension in your jaw, lips and throat open your mouth as widely as you can and yawn. Wriggle your jaw from side to side. Massage gently with your finger tips the place where your jaw hinges next to your ears. To lessen tension in your forehead massage your temples gently and the place between your eyebrows.

23. Focus on telling the story of your presentation rather than yourself. This shifts the energy from 'me' to 'message'. You'll find it does make a difference.

    The person who stands on both feet, head held high, chest exposed, and arms by side—we read these people as being open to experience the world. The person who hangs his head, folds his arms across his chest, crosses his legs and rolls his shoulders forward has closed himself off from experience. Their body says 'keep out'.

Leaning forward toward someone is interpreted as, I want to hear what you've got say. I'm interested. The expression 'had them sitting on the edge of their chairs' comes from an audience being so eager to hear what the speaker was saying they shifted as close as possible to them.

Leaning away from someone can be, 'I'm not sure. I'm taking some time out to think about it.'

Study excellence. A very effective way to teach yourself body language is to make a point of really noticing how successful speakers use their bodies. Get videos, and instead of listening to the speech, focus on their body language. Turn the sound off! When you turn it back on again, notice how speech and movement combine to create the whole impression.

9 Using Visual Aids and Props

Using Visual Aids as Notes

Simple visual aids can serve as your notes when speaking. Carefully select your titles. These titles alone can serve as "triggers" to what you want to say next. If you know your subject well and have rehearsed your presentation, your visual aids should be all you need to "jog" your memory. If you forget something that's okay; the audience would never know.

Using visual aids has 4 important advantages

1. You don't have to worry about what you're going to say next. Your next visual aid has your next major idea on it. Use effective titles that properly capture the main message of the visual aid.
2. Visual aids allow you to move around the room. Inexperienced speakers don't want to move around. Movement helps you to relax and adds energy to your presentations. Movement also allows the listeners to follow you and pay closer attention to you.
3. You can have good eye contact with your audience. You can look at your audience all the time, except when you look briefly at your visual aid. That's okay since the audience will also look at your visual aid. This will help them see your message as well as hear your message.

4. Your audience feels comfortable knowing you're on your planned track. Well-designed visual aids show that you have a plan and have properly prepared and you are following your plan.

Your visual aids don't have to be only word charts; they can include diagrams, pictures and graphs.

Note: When you use visual aids, always introduce your visual aid before you actually show the visual aid. Rehearse your presentation with your actual visual aids. It is very important that you are very familiar with your visual aids. Make sure your message and visual aids match. There is nothing worse than showing a visual aid that does not go along with what you are saying.

Practise using different transition phrases. For example: "Now that we have seen the ... let's look at ... "

"My next point deals with .... "

Your slides should have plenty of "white space" or "negative space." Do not feel compelled to fill empty areas on your slide with your logo or other unnecessary graphics or text boxes that do not contribute to better understanding. The less clutter you have on your slide, the more powerful your visual message will become.

Your presentation is for the benefit of the audience. But boring an audience with bullet point after bullet point is of little benefit to them. This brings us to the issue of text. The best slides may have no text at all. This may sound insane given the dependency of text slides today, but the best PowerPoint slides will be virtually meaningless with out the narration (that is you). Remember, the slides are meant to support the narration of the speaker, not make the speaker superfluous.

Many people often say something like this: "Sorry I missed your presentation. I hear it was great. Can you just send me your

Power-Point slides?" But if they are good slides, they will be of little use without you. Instead of a copy of your PowerPoint slides, it is far better to prepare a written document that highlights your content from the presentation and expands on that content. Audiences are much better served receiving a detailed, written handout as a takeaway from the presentation, rather than a mere copy of your PowerPoint slides. If you have a detailed handout or publication for the audience to be passed out after your talk, you need not feel compelled to fill your PowerPoint slides with a great deal of text.

Please remember to never, ever turn your back on the audience and read text from the slide word for word.

Use object builds and slide transitions judiciously. Object builds (also called animations), such as bullet points, should not be animated on every slide. Some animation is a good thing, but stick to the most subtle and professional (similar to what you might see on the evening TV news broadcast). A simple "Wipe Left-to-Right" (from the "Animations" menu) is good for a bullet point, but a "Move" or "Fly" for example is too tedious and slow (and yet, is used in many presentations today). Listeners will get bored very quickly if they are asked to endure slide after slide of animation. For transitions between slides, use no more than two-three different types of transition effects and do not place transition effects between all slides.

Use high-quality graphics including photographs. You can take your own high-quality photographs with your digital camera, purchase professional stock photography, or use the plethora of high-quality images available on line (be cautious of copyright issues, however). Never simply stretch a small, low-resolution photo to make it fit your layout, doing so will degrade the resolution even further.

Avoid using PowerPoint Clip Art or other cartoonish line art. Again, if it is included in the software, your audience has seen it a million times before. It may have been interesting in 1993, but today the inclusion of such clip art often undermines the professionalism of the presenter. There are exceptions, of course, and not all PowerPoint art is dreadful, but use carefully and judiciously.

You clearly need a consistent visual theme throughout your presentation, but most templates included in PowerPoint have been seen by your audience countless times (and besides, the templates are not all that great to begin with). Your audience expects a unique presentation with new (at least to them) content, otherwise why would they be attending your talk? No audience will be excited about a cookie-cutter presentation, and we must therefore shy away from any supporting visuals, such as the ubiquitous PowerPoint Design Template, that suggests your presentation is formulaic or prepackaged.

You can make your own background templates that will be more tailored to your needs. You can then save the PowerPoint file as a Design Template (.pot) and the new template will appear among your standard Microsoft templates for your future use. You can also purchase professional templates on-line (for example: www.powerpointtemplatespro.com).

Always be asking yourself, "How much detail do I need?" Presenters are usually guilty of including too much data in their on-screen charts. There are several ways to display your data in graphic form; here are a few things to keep in mind:

Pie Charts

Used to show percentages. Limit the slices to 4–6 and contrast the most important slice either with color or by exploding the slice.

Vertical Bar Charts

Used to show changes in quantity over time. Best if you limit the bars to 4-8.

Horizontal Bar Charts

Used to compare quantities. For example, comparing sales figures among the four regions of the company.

Line Charts

Used to demonstrate trends. For example, a simple line chart showing that our sales have gone up every year. The trend is good. The arrow comes in later to underscore the point: Our future looks good!

In general, tables are good for side-by-side comparisons of quantitative data. However, tables can lack impact on a visceral level. If you want to show how your contributions are significantly higher than two other parties, for example, it would be best to show that in the form of a bar chart. If you're trying to downplay the fact that your contributions are lower than others, however, a table will display that information in a less dramatic or emotional way.

Colour

Colour evokes feelings. Colour is emotional. The right colour can help persuade and motivate. Studies show that colour usage can increase interest and improve learning comprehension and retention.

You do not need to be an expert in colour theory, but it's good for business professionals to know at least a bit on the subject. Colours can be divided into two general categories: Cool (such as blue and green) and Warm (such as orange and red). Cool colours work best for backgrounds as they appear to recede away from us into the background. Warm colours generally work best for objects in the foreground (such as text) because they appear to be coming at us. It is no surprise, then, that the most ubiquitous PowerPoint slide colour scheme includes a blue background with yellow text. You do not need to feel compelled to use this colour scheme, though you may choose to use a variation of those colours.

If you will be presenting in a dark room (such as a large hall), then a dark background (dark blue, grey, etc.) with white or light text will work fine. But if you plan to keep most of the lights on (which is highly advisable) then a white background with black or dark text works much better. In rooms with a good deal of ambient light, a screen image with a dark background and light text tends to washout, but dark text on a light background will maintain its visual intensity a bit better.

Fonts

Fonts communicate subtle messages in and of themselves, which is why you should choose fonts deliberately. Use the same font set throughout your entire slide presentation, and use no more than two complementary fonts (e.g., Arial and Arial Bold). Make sure you know the difference between a Serif font (e.g., Times New Roman) and a Sans-Serif font (Helvetica or Arial). Serif fonts were designed to be used in documents filled with lots of text. Serif fonts are said to be easier to read at small point sizes, but for on screen presentations the serifs tend to get lost due to the relatively low resolution of projectors. San-serif fonts are generally best for PowerPoint presentations, but try to avoid the ubiquitous Helvetica. Regardless of what font you choose, make sure the text can be read from the back of the room.

Use video and audio when appropriate. Using video clips to show concrete examples promotes active cognitive processing, which is the natural way people learn. You can use video clips within PowerPoint without ever leaving the application or tuning on a VCR. Using a video clip not only will illustrate your point better, it will also serve as a change of pace, thereby increasing the interest of your audience. You can use audio clips (such as interviews) as well. Something to avoid, however, is cheesy sound effects that are included in PowerPoint (such as the sound of a horn or applause when transitioning slides). The use of superfluous sound effects attached to animations is a sure way to lose credibility with your audience.

The main benefits of learning how To use props are:

1. *Clarity:* You reduce the number of words you have to use to explain a concept or event. Remember that old saying, 'a picture is worth a thousand words'? Now think of the work a well-drawn graph or diagram does. Or what an aptly chosen photograph does to show a current event. The Hurricane Katrina pictures are an effective example. The devastation and misery wrought by the winds and flooding didn't need words. We saw and in seeing, felt it.
2. *Credibility:* You become more believable through your audience seeing something to reinforce your words. Another old saying says it for us like this: 'Seeing is believing'. When we add 'show' to 'tell' our credibility rating soars.

Does this mean every speech needs props to make it more effective? The short answer is, No. The longer answer is to consider carefully the nature of the speech you're preparing and its content.

Ask yourself: What could I show (or demonstrate) that would add value for my audience? Obviously, your answers will vary hugely. Do add any time or financial constraints into your decision making process. It takes time to prepare props to use effectively. It may take money as well. Weigh up the pros and cons before going ahead. If you don't have time, simplify your plans. It is better to have a few simple well-presented props than a grand incomplete scheme. You may even decide that this time, props are not for you.

How to Use Props

1. The best way is to integrate them into the body of your speech. It is more effective to show and tell as you go, rather than wait to the end of your speech and then show. By then

your audience may have forgotten why it is they are looking at your graph, photograph or grandmother clock!

2. Use clear descriptions of each item you use. Give enough information to satisfy interest without going on too long. You do not want to stop the flow of your speech by dwelling on one aspect.
3. Less IS more. Choose the BEST examples of whatever you've got to show. Less is more effective. Don't clutter an audience's minds with too many to take in.
4. Test before committing yourself to their use. Be sure the prop works in the venue. For example: If it's big, can it fit through the door, or on the stage ?
5. If you're using any electronic equipment to show photographs, graphs, etc., test it beforehand. Leave yourself enough time to familiarize yourself with how to operate it properly or to fix any problems you may find.
6. If you're reliant on someone else to operate equipment, be sure to rehearse fully with them. Give clear instructions about precisely what you want done, when. Have all your material in the right order ready for them. Prepare a 'cue sheet' for them to follow.
7. If you have a range of props to use throughout your speech, put them in order. Label them if necessary. Arrange them so they are easily picked up, put down and not in either your or your audience's way.
8. If you are demonstrating as well as showing, test and retest to make sure what you are doing is effective.

(What's the difference? Demonstrating is active. You are doing something. Showing is passive. You are holding something up to be looked at.

Example:

'Here's a remarkably easy drawing technique. I start here...' And the speaker does it on a drawing board in such a way to be visible to the audience.

'Here's the result of a drawing exercise...' And the speaker holds up his drawing pad to display the completed exercise.

The first is active and the second is passive.)

NB. When you demonstrate, the key is simplicity. Keep everything you do to a minimum. Think of how a live cooking demonstration is shown on television. Every aspect is prepared beforehand. The movements of the cook are clear and they've rehearsed their speech to fit precisely what they're doing so the audience can follow easily.

9. Thinking of using a live animal or pet? Think very carefully.

How will they respond to the stress of being moved?

How will they react to an unfamiliar place with lots of people?

Do you need a minder to look after them while you're talking?

If you do decide to go ahead, think every aspect out ahead and plan accordingly. Be real in your evaluation.

10. Sometimes our props need other people to demonstrate them. If that's the case for you, those people need to be part of your rehearsal process. They need to know what you're going to say, how you want them to react, where you want them to be on the stage (or where ever you're presenting), when you want them to come on and when to leave. And if you're going to have children taking part, make doubly sure they know what they're doing! Kids on stage with you can be great fun but the reverse is true too. It's up to you to make them feel at ease and confident about what you've asked them to do. Make it safe for them as well as yourself.

In summary, learning how to use props well will enhance how the audience receives your speech. It can give it the 'zing' factor.

10 Handling Q & A Sessions

Many presentations today are followed up with a question and answer period. To some people this can be the most exciting part of the presentation. To others it can be their worst nightmare. In fact, there are some presenters who purposely avoid the question and answer period all together. Below is provided a five-step approach to handling questions along with some additional tips to make your next question and answer session go smoother.

1. Listen to the entire question Listen to the entire question BEFORE you begin to answer any questions. Too many people start responding to a question before the entire question is even asked. Not waiting to hear the entire questions can result in you providing a response that had nothing to do with the question. Force yourself to LISTEN to the entire question and make sure you understand the question.
2. Pause and allow yourself time to value the question and listener. REPEAT the question out load so the entire audience can hear it. It is important that everyone "hear" the question or the answer you provide may not make sense to some of the people. By repeating the question, this will allow you some additional time to evaluate the question and formulate a response.
3. Credit the person for asking the question. You may say something like, "That was a great question" or, "Glad you

asked that question" or even, "I get asked that question by many people". A word of caution. If you credit one person with asking a question, be sure to credit EVERYONE for asking a question. You don't want people to feel their question was not as important.

4. Respond to the question honestly and the best you can. If you do NOT know an answer to a question, do not try to fake it. Be honest, and tell them you do not know but DO promise to research the answer for them and DO get back to them.

Bridge to the next question by asking them a question. "Does that answer your question?", "Is that the kind of information you were looking for?". This is critical. Once they respond to you, "YES" you now have permission to go on to the next person. This also gives them one more opportunity to say, "No" and allow them to clarify their question more by asking it again.

Some more tips on efficient handling of questions and answers sessions are given as follows:

1. Ask people to stand up when they ask a question. This does two things:
   a) It shows you more readily who is asking the question, and
   b) It makes it easier for the audience to also hear the question.
2. Have small sheets of paper available for people to write down their questions during your presentation. They may forget what they were going to ask earlier.
3. Allow people to pass the questions to you if they feel uncomfortable standing up and asking the question out loud. This gives the person who truly wants to ask a question an option.

4. Always repeat the question; this does three things:
   a) it makes sure you understood the question,
   b) it gives you a chance to value the question and think of an answer, and
   c) it assures the other people in the audience can hear the question since you are facing them.
5. Always take time to think "before" you answer all questions. This allows you time to think, especially for those difficult questions. Do the same for those questions you readily know the answer for. Responding too quickly to those questions you are most comfortable with will only bring attention to those questions you do not.
6. Have a pencil and paper available for you to write down questions you can't answer. You select someone to record the questions on paper. This way, you can properly follow up with the person who asked the question you couldn't answer. Be sure to get their name & phone number or address. Promise to get back to them and DO get back to them.